Saving
the
SNOWY
BRUMBIES

Saving
the
SNOWY
BRUMBIES

The Wilson sisters' adventures taming
horses from Australia's Snowy Mountains

Kelly Wilson

EBURY
PRESS

An Ebury Press book
Published by Penguin Random House Australia Pty Ltd
Level 3, 100 Pacific Highway, North Sydney NSW 2060
www.penguin.com.au

Penguin
Random House
Australia

First published in Australia by Ebury Press in 2017
First published in New Zealand by Penguin Random House in 2017

Addresses for the Penguin Random House group of companies can be found
at global.penguinrandomhouse.com/offices.

National Library of Australia
Cataloguing-in-Publication entry

Wilson, Kelly, author
Saving the snowy brumbies/Kelly Wilson

ISBN 978 0 14378 449 4 (paperback)

Wilson family
Wild horses – New South Wales – Snowy Mountains Region
Wild horse adoption – New Zealand – Kaimanawa Mountains
Horsemen and horsewomen – New Zealand
Snowy Mountains Region (N.S.W.)
Kaimanawa Mountains (North Island, N.Z.)

Cover design by Rachel Clark © Penguin Random House New Zealand
Cover photographs by Alexa Dodson and Kelly Wilson
Internal design by Rachel Clark © Penguin Random House New Zealand
Typeset in Australia by Post Pre-Press Group, Australia
Printed in Australia by Griffin Press, an accredited ISO AS/NZS 14001:2004
Environmental Management System printer

Penguin Random House Australia uses papers that are natural, renewable
and recyclable products and made from wood grown in sustainable forests.
The logging and manufacturing processes are expected to conform to the
environmental regulations of the country of origin.

This book is dedicated to the team at Isuzu Utes New Zealand, especially Murray, Gareth and Howard — thank you for your belief in us and for supporting our passions. You have become like family over the past two years and we can't thank you enough for understanding the compassion we have for wild horses, and for helping us to give them a voice. We hope that our journey with these horses inspires others to champion their cause and that instead of being seen as unwanted and unworthy by so many they will be recognised for their true worth. Without you, our work with the Brumbies couldn't have happened, so from the bottom of our hearts — thank you.

There was something special about seeing Brumbies in the wild — like having a childhood dream come true.

CONTENTS

INTRODUCTION

Living Legends

The history of the Brumbies, like that of all wild horses, it seems, is one of many contrasts. Once revered for their hardiness and embraced as a necessary part of Australia's high country, today these wild horses are in equal parts loved and hated. For many they are a symbol of the pioneering spirit of Australia, but for others they are little more than pests, damaging a delicate ecosystem that has not evolved to cope with being populated by so many horses.

The three of us — me and my sisters, Vicki and Amanda Wilson — have always been passionate about horses. Born and brought up in the upper North Island of New Zealand, we grew up reading the *Silver Brumby* series and watching the *The Man from Snowy River* — the Brumbies we read about were our first exposure to wild horses. As children we often pretended to be Brumbies, and would spend hours cantering around our yards at home, pretending to tame each other, or hiding from humans in the rock formations on neighbouring farmland — imagining we were in the Silver Brumbies' hidden canyon deep in the heart of the Snowy Mountains.

There wasn't a lot of spare money around when we were growing up, but our parents always supported us in our desire to own and train horses. When we were aged four (Amanda), seven (me) and nine (Vicki), we captured and tamed our very first wild ponies. The oldest of these were a palomino and a chestnut — we would often pretend that they were Thowra and Yarraman, the two most iconic stallions from the *Silver Brumby* stories. These books, which were written from the horses' point of view, gave us an appreciation of how scary each new situation must be for our own wild horses, and we strove to befriend them rather than forcing them into submission. Those early years working with young and feral horses gave us many of the skills we needed to succeed. From an early age we trained and competed ponies and horses in local competitions, progressing to showjumping on the New Zealand circuit with success at the highest levels. In between events we began to host camps and clinics on location and at our home property, Showtym Stables, teaching over 1000 riders a year, as well as breeding and training horses for both ourselves and others. Of the three of us, Vicki was (and still is) the most solely focused on her equestrian pursuits, having represented New Zealand a number of times in showjumping competitions. In 2016, while we were in Australia for the Brumby Challenge, Vicki was invited to compete in Road to the Horse — the World Championships of Colt Starting — which she won in convincing style, gaining her international recognition for her holistic approach to horsemanship. Amanda, while just as successful as Vicki in the competition arena, became equally as passionate about film and writing; and when I was not riding, writing or photographing, I would spend as much time as possible travelling and adventuring.

Our work with truly wild horses began in 2012, when Watch Me Move, a showjumping pony that we had initially bought and trained, won the biggest Pony Grand Prix event in the Southern Hemisphere. When we purchased Watch Me Move we were told he had been born wild in some of the most rugged mountains of New Zealand — the Kaimanawa Ranges. Following his win, his rider, Tegan Newman, and the three of us were invited down to the Kaimanawa Ranges by Kaimanawa Heritage Horses (who advocate for the welfare and care of the Kaimanawas) to view the herds in the wild. For the first time we became aware of the plight of our nation's wild horses.

Over the previous 20 years, thousands of horses had been culled in an effort to reduce the population from 2000 and thereby protect the sensitive ecological area where the wild horses lived; by the time we became involved, the culling was maintained through musters every second year to keep the population at about 300. Because of negative stereotyping and a massive lack of public awareness surrounding the Kaimanawas, most of the mustered horses were being sent to slaughter. Hoping that we could do something to help, we saved 11 horses from the 2012 muster and documented their journey to domestication. I wrote a book, *For the Love of Horses*, about our own journey to become showjumpers, trainers and, eventually, tamers of wild Kaimanawas, which became a best-seller.

In 2013, following my twin passions for horses and photography, I spent some time photographing Walers and Brumbies in Australia, and visited the Victorian Brumby Association to see first-hand many of the Brumbies they had saved from slaughter. Having tamed our first Kaimanawas just 10 months before, all three of us were personally invested in and passionate about the plight of wild horses in our home country — and seeing the Australian equivalent opened my eyes to the plight of wild horses on an international scale.

Another three years passed before we again crossed paths with the Australian Brumbies. During this time so much had changed in our lives. Our focus during the competition season was on our showjumpers, with Vicki and Amanda competing to World Cup level on their most successful horses Showtym Cassanova, Showtym Cadet MVNZ and Ngahiwi Showtym Premier. During the winter months our work with wild horses continued — in 2014 we saved another 12 Kaimanawas from that year's muster, and our work taming them featured in the hit television show *Keeping Up With The Kaimanawas* and my second book, *Stallion Challenges*. While every wild horse that we work with holds a special place in our hearts, there were two Kaimanawas in particular that became an integral part of our family: Argo, a young stallion trained by Vicki, and the veteran stallion Elder, who was the most challenging of any wild horse we have tamed. While Argo was ridden for the first time just eight days out of the wild, it took more than 500 days for Elder to reach the same milestone — something that we achieved through endless patience and trust, rather than force, in an effort to produce happy horses that enjoy their lives with us.

Through our work with New Zealand's wild Kaimanawas, in 2015 we were invited to compete in the prestigious Extreme Mustang Makeover in America. Along with Alexa and Kirsty (two of the girls who worked with us taming horses, showjumping and managing our busy lives), we spent three months taming 11 wild Mustangs and taking them on a 5000-kilometre road trip around the Wild West. Out of this came another documentary, filmed and produced by Amanda, and another best-selling book, *Mustang Ride*, written by me.

Somehow we had gone from being passionate people with a love of horses to being role models with a purpose — giving wild horses a voice, especially the tens of thousands that face either captivity or death when their freedom is taken from them at the hands of humans. Our work with wild horses had taken a global turn, and with every adventure our interest in them grew. Late in 2015, a phone call from the Victorian Brumby Association gave us pause. The Brumbies were in dire trouble and the association wanted to know if we would be interested in learning more about their plight — and also training some wild Brumbies as part of the Australian Brumby Challenge. The event was very similar to the Extreme Mustang Makeover and our home-grown Kaimanawa Stallion Challenges: in the Australian version of the challenge, trainers have 150 days to train a wild Brumby before competing at Equitana (a major event on the Australian equestrian calendar). Started by the Victorian Brumby Association (VBA) in 2014, the challenge was designed to showcase the trainability of wild Brumbies in front of 40,000 people, and raise awareness about their plight, before the horses were sold off by public auction at the event.

Intrigued, we started asking questions, and quickly discovered that the Brumbies' situation was even worse than that of their American and New Zealand counterparts. Australia has a huge number of horses roaming wild, resulting in large numbers being culled every year. Because of our success in bringing the plight of other wild horses to the attention of the public and, in New Zealand, increasing re-homing numbers to the point where every Kaimanawa suitable for re-homing was saved from the 2016 muster, the VBA hoped that our involvement would generate additional publicity for the Brumbies, who were in desperate need of champions.

From the moment we turned our attention to Australia's wild horses, we began learning as much as we could. As with the Kaimanawas and Mustangs before we became involved with them, we knew little about these living legends — apart from there being a lot of them. When we began digging deeper, we discovered just how many wild horses there were in Australia, and how many were being culled each year. The numbers were staggering. New Zealand's population of Kaimanawas is kept at about 300 by a biennial muster, with 150 or so looking for homes every two years. In America, 45,000 Mustangs roam wild and about 50,000 are captive in holding yards, in need of an immediate solution. But in Australia, an estimated 400,000 to 1 million Brumbies roam wild, and well over 100,000 are culled each year. Worse, rather than being rounded up for re-homing, almost all of the Brumbies are either aerially culled (shot from helicopters) or sent to slaughter after mustering or trapping, an unsustainable solution that barely controls their numbers.

What shocked us most were some of the ways in which the culling was done. Many of the old-fashioned culling and capturing methods that we'd read about in old-fashioned books as children were *not* a thing of the past — they were still very much happening in Australia. In some areas, Brumbies were still being trapped by the hundreds, lassoed and chased on horseback, broncoed to exhaustion like rodeo steeds, hunted with bow and arrows, or shot from helicopters by the thousands. To top things off, just recently the New South Wales government had proposed culling 90 per cent of the wild horses in the Snowy Mountains through the use of ground shooting, where the horses would be culled by people on foot and the carcasses left to rot where they fall.

Without going to Australia, we couldn't be sure whether our research was more fiction or fact, so we decided to take up the invitation. Keeping our minds open in the hope that the situation wasn't as bad as it seemed, we began organising both the time and the funding to make it possible. The networks that had aired *Keeping Up With The Kaimanawas* on both sides of the Tasman to over half a million viewers were interested in a second season, this time following our work with the Brumbies. This was excellent news — media coverage on mainstream television throughout New Zealand and Australia, along with a book that I'd write, had every chance of enabling the Brumbies to gain the love of the Australian public, much like Kiwis had embraced our own Kaimanawas. We couldn't wait for our adventures with the Brumbies to begin.

CHAPTER 1

Wild Ride

Our work with the Brumbies, and the ripple effects that it led to, almost never happened. In those final months before we left New Zealand, we were frantically busy with the showjumping season along with writing scripts and training horses to create a theatrical show depicting our history of taming wild horses — and nearly everything that could have gone wrong *did* go wrong.

Just a few months before we were due to leave for Australia — and just an hour before we were due to perform our show in front of a sold-out stadium of 4000 people — Vicki was knocked over by a horse in our final practice. Badly concussed and barely conscious, Vicki was rushed to hospital. We were thrown into crisis mode, with the organisers frantically trying to work out a way to cancel the show without upsetting the thousands of spectators. Flustered but sure we could still pull off a good show, Amanda, Alexa and I banded together and quickly reassigned the various roles. Alexa would play Vicki, and Amanda and I would share the roles in those scenes where Alexa had originally featured. Fortunately, Alexa had helped me write the original script and knew all the lines. With just an hour to go to curtain-raise, we reshuffled all the scenes and learnt the riding routines we would need. I would ride Vicki's World Cup showjumper Showtym Cadet MVNZ in a formation ride during a war scene, Alexa would be cueing horses to rear and lie down, Amanda would be riding Vicki's Kaimanawa, Argo, in a scene involving working bareback and bridleless, and Kirsty would ride Showtym Spotlight to open the show. Our biggest problem was that the horses had only been trained by Vicki — and with no time left to practise we weren't sure how well it would all work.

Luckily the show was a huge hit; although some of the horses got confused by being handled and ridden by someone new, everything else went better than we could have dreamed. Vicki even made it back in time to get a photo with the crew, although she looked a little the worse for wear. The feedback was overwhelmingly positive and people lined up for hours to meet us after the show; we were even asked to take it on a nationwide tour and seriously considered doing just that, as we felt that Vicki had missed out on the experience of a lifetime. It had been an incredible thing to be a part of. Most importantly, the night had highlighted how special New Zealand's wild horses were and paid tribute to the special Kaimanawas that had sparked our own journey with them.

The next few weeks were hard on Vicki: along with days of memory loss, her head injury gave her debilitating headaches, and it was a long time before she felt ready to ride again. We knew she was in a bad way when she voluntarily decided to miss the New Zealand Horse of the Year show, especially during what had been a hugely successful season for her. Amanda represented the family, finishing second on Showtym Cassanova in the Olympic Cup, the most prestigious event of the year. She used the prize money to be reunited with Bragg, her favourite American Mustang, whom she brought over from America.

Then, just days after the competition, we received bad news from the local television network: insufficient funding had come through for the second TV series, partly because of the lack of New Zealand content, and they were forced to drop the show. Without television our work with the Brumbies would reach significantly fewer people, but we were still determined to raise awareness of the horses' plight. Confident that in this digital age a web series could be even more successful than a TV series, as it would allow ready access for people from every corner of the globe, we strove to get the funding needed for a production team to follow our progress. Unfortunately, our efforts were entirely unsuccessful, and just a week before we were due to leave for Australia we had to sit down and contemplate our options.

There were really only two, and neither was ideal. We could head to Australia alone and completely unfunded; or we could pull out. The timing of the Brumby Challenge was part of the problem — we were still in the middle of taming the Kaimanawas we'd saved a month earlier after the 2016 muster, and were also preparing our team of showjumpers for competition. It was never going to be practical or feasible to be based in Australia for five months to train Brumbies, so instead we'd planned to spend only a part of our time there — about 30 days in Australia and the remaining 120 back in New Zealand. The TV production company had budgeted for flying the Brumbies back to New Zealand to make it possible for us to work with them; return flights for the horses were too costly for us to manage ourselves (although we could cover the other costs). On top of this, Vicki — our most experienced trainer — was still suffering from bad headaches. Pulling out completely wasn't the ideal solution, but it was the most sensible. We still wanted to go — we were sure that we could still make an impact without a *Keeping Up With The Brumbies* series, but everything just seemed to be stacked against us.

When our sponsors, Isuzu Utes New Zealand, heard about our dilemma, they offered to pay the costs of the horses' flights to ensure that our work with Australia's wild horses could continue. This was a very generous offer, but not wanting to spend their money unwisely we thought long and hard about why we were wanting to work with the Brumbies. Finally, confident that it was for the right reasons — solely to benefit the wild horses — we gratefully took Isuzu up on their offer. Alexa, who was originally planning to compete but had given up the idea as she couldn't justify the extra cost, decided to join us anyway (although wouldn't be competing). Within days we were at the airport, en route to Australia and the beginning of a new adventure.

WE ARRIVED AT THE BRUMBY JUNCTION SANCTUARY at Glenlogie, a three-hour drive northwest of Melbourne, just on sunset and, I have to be honest, we were quite disappointed with our first impression of the Brumbies assigned to us. They were smaller and plainer than we'd expected; there were certainly no creamies like the legendary Thowra among them, and they were also smaller than the wild Kaimanawas and Mustangs we had tamed previously. As darkness set in — early because it was the middle of June, at the start of winter — we quickly fed hay to our new charges and then ventured into our cabin to warm up, unpack and talk. Mostly we were questioning why, of the hundreds of thousands of wild horses all across Australia, these specific Brumbies had been chosen to represent the breed. Of course we had no answer to this, so soon fell asleep.

The next morning, we got bundled up in scarves and headed outside to brave the cold, eager to see our Brumbies in the light. Twenty-seven horses and their trainers were competing in the Australian Brumby Challenge, and all but six trainers had collected their Brumbies the previous day. In the yards were just the three mares assigned to us and a yearling for the youth challenge, who was getting collected later that day. The other two Brumbies — almost-identical black mares with big white faces — had been turned out into paddocks until their trainers could arrive to collect them a couple of weeks later.

Our second impressions of the heights of our mares weren't much better than the first; the last time we'd ridden ponies this small, we'd been young children. Amanda's bay mare was a tiny wee thing, standing less than 13 hands high; she eyed us warily, leaping forward and spinning when someone accidentally banged against the rail. Although small, she was very striking and, apart from her size, Amanda was impressed by her type. The chestnut that was assigned to me was about 13.2 hands, with only a few white markings. Nondescript was the word that came to mind — a small pony that was plain in both colour and looks. Not a horse to catch your eye, she seemed to fade into the background as she stood quietly in a corner of her yard, ignoring us.

Vicki's Brumby was the biggest of the three, standing at about 14 hands, and slight in build. She was beautiful, with a rare and striking bronze colouring, but grey flecks around her eyes and a generally poor condition hinted at her being the oldest of them all, bringing its own problems. Unlike my mare, she paced restlessly, stressed about humans being so close; Amanda and I were both relieved that she hadn't been assigned to us.

We were to be based at the Brumby sanctuary for the whole time we would be in Australia. Privately owned and funded, the sanctuary consists of two 50-acre paddocks where wild Brumbies roam in herds during their initial transition period, with the remaining land fenced into smaller paddocks and yards where other horses are kept in training. The VBA, also based at the sanctuary, was formed in 2007 after several years of informal Brumby rescue. Their main goals struck a chord with us: to rescue and re-home wild Brumbies; help develop humane, sustainable and effective management systems; and educate the general public — showing them what Brumbies actually are, and how the same qualities that make them successful wild horses also mean that they are eminently suited to domestication. Since 2007 the VBA has tamed, trained and re-homed more than 480 Brumbies, which have gone on to be very successful in a variety of disciplines.

Colleen O'Brien, the property owner and also the president of the VBA, soon joined us at the rails and, while watching the horses, we asked her questions about our three. All of the Brumbies competing in the Australian Brumby Challenge were from the Snowy Mountains, which stretch from Victoria through to New South Wales. Amanda's mare, along with most of the black Brumbies, was from the Bogong High Plains; our other two were from Kosciuszko National Park. Like all the other horses competing in the Australian Brumby Challenge, they were coming to us completely untouched.

Colleen told us that the National Parks and Wildlife Services (NPWS) were currently capturing about 600–800 Brumbies each year from Kosciuszko, passively trapping them at various sites on and around Long Plain Road. While many were chestnuts, there were also plenty of roans, blacks, bays and greys in the region, and also the occasional palomino. Each week during the winter months, the trapped Brumbies were available for re-homing. Only about 11 per cent are saved, sadly;

the rest go to 'dogger dealers' who sell them for meat. The smaller ones tend to go to local knackeries, while some of the larger ones have been known to travel on trucks for up to nine weeks to be slaughtered on the docks and exported to Europe for human consumption. It wasn't unheard of for the more aggressive stallions to have sacks forced over their heads to make the trip in darkness so that bite marks wouldn't mar the other horses' flesh and make the meat less desirable.

We asked Colleen whether our assigned Brumbies represented the average colour and size of the horses that roam in the Snowy Mountains; she shook her head. Her reply answered many of the questions we'd had the previous night. After making the seven-hour journey to the holding yards to save a truckload of wild horses, Colleen had arrived to find only small ones left. The meat sellers had already been through the yards and taken out the biggest horses, for which they would get the most money. Along with the smallest of the adults, those left in the yards were foals and weanlings. Colleen had a tough decision to make; her truck would fit only 10 horses and there were more than 40 still in the yards — and since it was Friday and no wild horses were kept over the weekend, any horse she didn't save would be on its way to the local abattoir by nightfall.

Colleen had to override her emotions and be sensible about selecting the horses she believed would have the best chance of settling into domestication and being re-homed. For her, the most important factors were temperament and conformation, but she also knew how important size and looks were to potential owners. A horse with lots of white markings would be more appealing, and sometimes this was enough to differentiate between which ones to save.

Although my mare, who was heavily pregnant at the time, was one of the plainest in the yards, she stood out because of her relaxed demeanour, seeming unconcerned about the people watching her — she was the first to be chosen. Colleen had also selected a few other pregnant mares and a number of young foals who would soon forget their wild beginnings and transition to domestication much more easily than adult horses that had run free for years. With all but one horse chosen, Colleen's eight-year-old daughter, Bridie, had pointed to Vicki's mare nervously pacing in the far corner and begged to save her; Bridie was convinced that the mare was from the same family as her own Brumby, Millie, as they were so similar in colour. Colleen agreed, and the park rangers set about sorting out the chosen ones. As Colleen drove away with a truck loaded with Brumbies, she had to shake off the heartbreak of knowing the fate of those left behind.

Vicki and I looked at our Brumbies, seeing them in a new light; rather than their size being a negative thing, unrepresentative of the breed, we now saw it for the positive it was. In a world where big means being sold for meat and small means a chance at being saved, they were indeed the lucky ones. Our Brumbies' small stature was a constant and vivid reminder of the fate that befalls the majority of Snowy Brumbies culled each year.

Amanda's mare had a different story; she had never been destined for slaughter. Years earlier the VBA had committed to saving every Brumby that was trapped in the Bogong High Plains, since only 125 horses live in this region. Most are bay or black with white markings, ranging in size from 12.2 hands through to 15 hands. While Amanda's mare was at the smaller end of the scale, she was a fairly good example of the genetically isolated Bogong Brumbies.

Knowing the history of the horses was hugely important to us developing an emotional attachment to each one — something that is vital when working with wild horses. Entering the yards, we quietly separated them so that we could begin working with them. Vicki's mare, who hadn't stopped pacing since we had first seen her, grew highly agitated when Vicki stood in the centre of her yard, and circled her, unsettled. Moving to the gate, Vicki left the yard to give the bronze mare more room, but it had little effect. She continued to show stress, pacing along the far fence line, and never once took her eyes off Vicki, whom she obviously perceived as a threat.

Hoping that Vicki's mare would settle down with fewer people around, Amanda and I left to work with our own horses. My mare stood quietly with her head lowered; although she appeared quiet, it was obvious that she was uncomfortable with her situation and I was careful to give her the time she needed to process my presence. Amanda's bay was the bravest of the three, boldly approaching her a number of times before her courage failed her and she darted back to her corner. For the next half-hour, Amanda and I stood in our horses' yards barely moving; the occasional raising of one hand or the shifting of a shoulder was enough to gain their interest. At first they would just flick an ear towards us; later, once they had become more attuned to our body language, they would turn to face us. At once we would softly step back, while praising the horses with our voices. Stepping back from the horses was a way of rewarding them, by reducing the threat of us being so close to them. From a young age we found that horses, especially wild ones, respond well to a relationship built on trust and friendship, so we have developed this quiet and gentle approach to taming them.

Satisfied with their progress at this initial meeting, we left them and moved to the raceway to watch Vicki's Brumby. The mare hadn't stopped moving once in the hour since we'd arrived at the yards to feed and muck out, and although Vicki hadn't shifted from her spot leaning against the rails the mare was still on high alert; sweat was starting to show on her coat. Not wanting to cause her further distress, we all left as soon as the mare paused, even though it was only for a fraction of a second, and headed out to see the other Brumbies on the property. We were keen to see and learn as much about these wild horses as possible.

CHAPTER 2

High Alert

As we walked from paddock to paddock, visiting wild horses at varying stages of their training, we were interested to see the range of types and colours. A stunning silver roan gelding, standing at 15 hands high, caught our eye; in the next paddock over, a handsome bay roan watched us warily. Both were from Kosciuszko and looked more like what we had been expecting for our own Brumbies in terms of size and colour.

In one paddock of mares and foals, one foal was very thin, with every rib visible. When we pointed him out, Colleen sighed heavily and told us his story. It wasn't pretty. The foal had been mustered from the wild in the deserts of the Northern Territory and then been trucked with his herd all the way down to Petersburg in South Australia to be slaughtered for meat. Due to their size, Brumby foals aren't worth much to the meat sellers. To save having to feed extra, low-value horses, this particular truck driver, who had unloaded the horses at holding yards overnight, was planning to shoot the foals out from under their mothers at daybreak before reloading the mares and stallions and continuing on the journey.

Someone had overheard him talking about this, and snuck out in the dark to rustle the foals away from the mares — managing to steal away with four of the youngest. Too young to be weaned, and traumatised by the experience of being mustered and trucked, three of the wild Brumby foals had died trying to transition to bottled milk. The fourth one was so weak that its rescuer loaded it up and drove it to the VBA in the hope that they would have the experience needed to save it. When the foal had first arrived at the sanctuary he had been skin and bone, but now, three months later, his condition had improved a little and he was enjoying a herd situation and supplemented feed. Colleen told us that shooting the foals like this was a common practice among truck drivers transporting wild horses for meat; it was a sickening story.

As we watched the foal interacting with the other horses, we questioned Colleen about the Desert Brumbies. It had taken us a while to realise that the Snowy Brumbies we were working with were just a small, genetically isolated group and represented only a very small percentage of Australia's Brumby population. It had been hard initially to understand why there was so much fuss about 800 of the 6000 horses in Kosciuszko being culled each year (and the New South Wales government's plan to exterminate 90 per cent — 5400 — of them); we'd heard that 20 times that number were being killed annually across Australia and had been for years. Were our facts wrong, or were they horrifyingly right and the general public had no idea of the fate that was befalling their iconic horses? We felt that we needed to weave together a proper understanding of the sheer scale of the problem.

Only 10,000 wild horses live in New South Wales and Victoria, with about 6000 of those living in the Snowy Mountains. Another 20,000 live in Queensland, the number having dropped significantly over the past decade, where more than 6000 Brumbies were shot during government aerial culls. Most of the rest, estimated at anywhere between 370,000 and 970,000, roam throughout the sparsely populated and harsh environments of the Northern Territory, South Australia and Western Australia. (The higher estimate comes from the government, which has the job of managing the wild populations; Brumby activists claim that the lower estimate is more realistic.) Privately owned stations, some hundreds of thousands of acres in size, have become the home of the majority of Australia's wild horses; vast expanses of desert land, barely able to sustain stock, mean that in severe droughts the Brumbies often die in huge numbers from starvation or lack of water. In an attempt to control numbers, the state and federal governments send out helicopters to do counts; if a particular ranch is overrun then a letter of compliance is sent out demanding that the owners remove a set number of animals, often numbering in the thousands. Refusing to comply means that the helicopters will return for an aerial cull and a hefty bill will be sent to the land-owners. Instead, mustering the herds and trucking them to the abattoir is often a more cost-effective solution, but in some regions this isn't possible due to a lack of road access — and thousands of Brumbies are shot down from the skies.

Unlike the herds in the Snowy Mountains, the Desert Brumbies are a range of completely different types, sizes and colours. Brumbies of every colour, including pinto, are often seen, and horses as large as 16.2 hands have been caught. In the early twentieth century, some station owners purposely released pedigree sires into the wild herds to improve the quality and size of the horses, making them more desirable as ridden horses for use as stock horses and in the cavalry. After World War I the demand for ridden horses decreased, and in the following years machines increasingly replaced horses in farming. Across Australia, unwanted horses were often set free, increasing the feral populations that were first recorded in folklore and history books in the early 1800s.

Like in America, where the wild horses are descended from animals brought to the New World by the Spanish in the sixteenth century, only the sturdiest horses survived the initial trip by ship to Australia, resulting in a hardy horse that thrived in difficult conditions. In the 200 years since they first escaped or were released into the wild, their numbers escalated rapidly, and they have now become the largest wild horse population in the world. Their situation is not unlike that of Australia's population of feral camels. Like the Brumbies, the camels were also shipped to Australia during the nineteenth century, to provide transport during the construction and colonising of central and western Australia. They were released to turn wild at a similar time to the horses, for similar reasons; and being well adapted to desert conditions their numbers also grew rapidly. At their peak, in 2008, the number of camels was believed to have reached over 1 million (although this figure was later revised downwards); the following year, A$19 million was set aside for a four-year project to reduce the population to 300,000 through a mixture of aerial culling, ground culling and mustering. Unsurprisingly, feral camel numbers are on the rise again.

Trying to get our reeling minds around these numbers, we moved on to visit the wild Brumby herds in the far pastures of the sanctuary. Here, old stallions, long since gelded but unsuitable for re-homing due to injury or their advanced age, were run with herds of wild mares during their transition period. For the first 18 months after being trapped and saved, pregnant mares run wild at the sanctuary, enjoying the freedom and safety of a 50-acre paddock; they continue to live in a herd situation until they've given birth and have had their foals weaned. The younger stallions, frequently selected to compete in the Australian Brumby Challenge, get nine months of transition time. After arriving at the sanctuary they are sedated in a crush and gelded, given time to recover in yards and then moved to the 50-acre paddocks in bachelor herds while their testosterone levels drop. Living in the paddocks also gives the horses the opportunity to become accustomed to fences and artificial water sources. In many ways, this management of the Brumbies was the perfect median between the Kaimanawas, who came to us totally wild directly from the government-funded helicopter musters, and the Mustangs, who were kept yarded for years on end in what were essentially feed lots.

Saving the Brumbies that come through the VBA sanctuary means a huge long-term commitment, with 9 to 18 months of feeding being invested in them. To help pay for it all, most Brumbies have sponsors who contribute to the basic costs; there is no government funding. Naming the Brumbies is part of the sponsorship deal; my mare had been named VBA Shyla, meaning daughter of the mountain, and Vicki's was called VBA Diana — although, due to her colouring, we soon gave her the paddock name Arana, meaning moon. Amanda's mare had never been sponsored, so Amanda spent much time brainstorming a name and eventually settled on VBA Ballarat, meaning resting place, in remembrance of the thousands of Snowy Brumbies that had lost their lives over the years. Ballarat was also the name of the closest town to the Brumby sanctuary (about 45 minutes' drive away).

AFTER LUNCH WE HEADED BACK OUTSIDE TO work with the Brumbies again. As soon as we left our cabin, which was in sight of the yards, we noticed movement; Arana had remained on high alert and had started running around as soon as she saw us. It was an interesting reaction, something we'd rarely seen in other horses. We have found that most wild horses have a natural curiosity about humans, but Arana had a deep-seated mistrust of people and genuinely seemed to think that her life was in danger when they were around. Rather than working with her, Vicki leant on the fence to watch her again, hoping that she'd settle down in time. Fortunately, Shyla, who was yarded between Arana and Ballarat, wasn't upset by the stressed mare beside her, so I was able to begin working with her. Even with a fence separating us, Arana paced restlessly, snorting as she alternated between watching Vicki and watching me working with Shyla. Although this situation was enough to put any horse on edge, Shyla remained as steady as a rock and I could see why her temperament had saved her all those months ago. There was something quite remarkable about her.

On my other side, I heard Amanda laugh as she worked with Ballarat, and turned to watch the little Brumby trot towards her and stamp her hoof before darting back and then repeating the process. Amused by her antics, Amanda patiently allowed the mare to approach and retreat as she wished, letting the mare choose the timing and the distance. Ballarat's boldness gave her the confidence to gradually creep closer each time, and it wasn't long before she was standing in front of Amanda, close enough to be touched. Amanda slowly raised her hand, reaching out quietly, but the mare started, leaping sideways before cantering back to a corner. Although brave, she was incredibly reactive and it took a while before she got up enough courage to approach Amanda again.

Turning my attention back to my own Brumby, I began asking more of her; while she remained quiet, she did her best to ignore me, lowering her head and turning away slightly as a way of coping. My priority was to get her comfortable enough around me to raise her head and look at me again — until she was willing to acknowledge me, I knew she wouldn't be ready to be approached, touched or haltered. I asked her to walk out on a circle (by holding one hand out in the direction I wanted her to go, and gently waving the other one to encourage her to move), and then stepped in front of her as she moved to encourage her to turn in and face me. The first few times she turned away instead, pressing closer to the fence instead of taking any steps towards me, but I repeated the movements until she stepped in towards me as she turned. I backed up, pleased, then again repeated the movements a few more times until she was standing quietly, watching me, with both eyes focused on me for the first time. Pleased with her progress, I quietly backed out of the yard and was thrilled to see her turn to watch me as I left.

Giving our mares a break, Amanda and I went to watch Vicki as she entered Arana's yard. Since people would be a part of Arana's daily life from now on, Vicki wanted the mare to become accustomed to people being in her space and to realise that we weren't there to hurt her. Rather than pacing against the far fence line, this time the mare took off at a canter, circling around Vicki and snorting with stress as she warily bolted around the yard. To make herself as unintimidating as possible, Vicki stood completely still, looking down at the ground; nothing about her position or her body language was threatening. For 10 minutes Arana cantered, her coat becoming slick with sweat, and still she showed no signs of slowing. Vicki waited patiently; after a while, Arana changed to a trot and then eventually a walk and, finally, some 40 minutes after Vicki had first entered the yard, a halt. Vicki gently glanced up at the mare — and although she'd moved only a fraction it was enough to upset Arana and send her cantering off again. This time, though, it was only a few minutes before she stood still, watching Vicki tensely. Vicki quietly backed from the yard to give Arana time to relax — she'd had more than enough human interaction for one day. Apart from Memo, an older Kaimanawa mare from the 2012 muster, Arana was the only wild horse we had encountered that had instinctively run when a person had entered its yard. Again watching from the fence, Vicki quietly mulled over her and Arana's options.

Before leaving the yards, Amanda and I returned to our horses to spend a few more minutes with them. Arana was so easily distracted that we hadn't wanted to worry her by working the other Brumbies within her sight, and we'd been careful to keep very still while Vicki was in the yard with her. Shyla and Ballarat had already impressed us today so we made the session very short. My aim was to see whether Shyla would eat hay out of my hand. I crouched low in the centre of the yard with the hay held out, and gradually Shyla plucked up enough courage to step forward and eat from my outstretched fingers. Considering that she'd had unlimited hay available all day, her action was definitely a matter of choice and I was pleased at how much confidence she'd gained from the hour I'd spent with her over the course of the day.

Meanwhile, Amanda's Brumby was standing in front of her and stretching her head out to be touched. Over the next few minutes the curious mare would let herself be patted, then would stamp her hoof and dart backwards, only to step forward and repeat the process a few seconds later. Amanda was grinning, pleased with how well Ballarat was progressing; I was equally happy with my own mare.

CHAPTER 3

Brumby-run?

The following day, Alexa was paired up with the striking bay roan gelding we'd seen on our tour. He was called Ranger and had been trapped two years earlier. Although Alexa wouldn't be competing in the Australian Brumby Challenge, this gave her a horse to focus on during our time in Australia and she was looking forward to winning him over. Unlike our Brumbies, Ranger wasn't completely unhandled; he had been re-homed but was then returned to the VBA with behavioural issues. He had been back at the sanctuary for six months, left untouched, and now genuinely feared humans. Working with horses that have been misunderstood or mistreated in the past is always worrying; you never really know when or what went wrong, or how much handling they actually had.

After a lot of patience, Alexa managed to get a halter on Ranger that first day, but in many ways he was more challenging than our fully wild Brumbies. Colleen had a good point to make about the handling of wild horses: if a wild horse is mistreated or rushed in its initial handling, then 100 per cent of its experience with humans is negative; whereas if a domesticated horse suddenly has a handler or rider mistreat it, it has a whole library of good experiences to default back to and will be far more forgiving. We couldn't help agreeing. Because a wild horse has nothing positive to compare its treatment with, a poor experience with humans will naturally lead to it perceiving people in a negative light.

While we were watching Alexa work with Ranger, Vicki's mare

started running around her yard again. While not as stressed as the day before, it was obvious that she was upset at having humans within sight. Watching her, Colleen commented that the only other horses that mentally fragile she'd seen were the first 130 Brumbies the VBA had saved, all of which had been Brumby-run from the Alpine National Park in Victoria. Vicki immediately asked for more information, because the mare's behaviour was completely unlike anything we'd seen before; if Arana had previously had a bad experience with humans, it would explain a lot.

As we listened, our concern grew. In Brumby running, a rider on horseback uses dogs to find and chase wild horses, often to the point of exhaustion, until the rider is able to catch up and lasso one. Younger Brumbies give up more quickly, while the older ones become quite cunning, darting through the under-brush to escape capture. Young, weak, thin or pregnant mares are the most vulnerable and are generally the easiest to capture.

While Brumby running (under different names) was once used throughout the world for capturing horses — including the Kaimanawas and the Mustangs — most countries have now banned the chasing, harassment and capture of wild horses in this manner. Unfortunately, in Australia there seems to be a way around the ban. Although it is illegal for the general public to capture wild Brumbies, the Victorian government contracts Brumby runners to capture a set quota of wild horses each year as a method of controlling their numbers. While historically Brumby running was done for sport, the contracts have turned it into a money-making venture for the horsemen who are sent in to lasso Brumbies; each rider often setting out to catch up to six horses per day. Most Brumby runners end up getting paid double, by dropping off the traumatised horses at local abattoirs on their way home and collecting the money for their meat.

Like the meat sellers, Brumby runners prefer the bigger Brumbies. In one incident, a horseman caught 26 Brumbies over the course of a single day, capturing them one at a time and tying them to trees. Once his six lassos had all been used, he backtracked and released the four smallest animals and went out to catch another four. He repeated this until eventually he had six Brumbies that were large enough to fetch good meat prices. One by one he would drag each horse back to his truck, with the horses fighting the rope that held them until they were too exhausted to struggle. And it didn't end there — the frightened horses were dragged onto the truck with a boat winch. When they were finally unloaded in the slaughter pens, their bodies would have been so damaged from struggling against the ropes that they probably wouldn't have been much use for anything other than meat.

While those horses that were dropped off at an abattoir after capture had a brutal fate, the other Brumbies, those that had been caught and then released as too small, weren't necessarily the lucky ones. Many would have had nasty rope burns and virtually all would have developed a fear of humans, having learnt to flee quickly when they saw riders approaching. When Colleen first began rescuing wild Brumbies destined for slaughter, she had assumed that all wild horses were as difficult to tame because she thought that Brumby running was the way all of them were captured. It wasn't until she re-homed some passively trapped Brumbies from the Snowy Mountains that she realised there was a kinder way, one that minimised both the physical and the mental damage done to the horses. These passively trapped Brumbies were significantly easier to tame and more responsive to the halter and lead.

Answering a question from Vicki, Colleen said that it was possible that Arana had been Brumby-run. Although the practice was illegal in New South Wales where Arana had roamed, being considered an inhumane method of managing the Brumbies, it wasn't unheard of for people in the high country to illegally run wild Brumbies for sport; it had long been a tradition there.

Regardless of whether Arana had been Brumby-run or not, the mare was certainly in need of lots of patience. Both that afternoon and the next morning, she began circling as soon as Vicki re-entered her yard, as agitated as she'd been during their first session. Since Arana had such a pronounced flight response and was working herself into exhaustion, Vicki decided to get her into the crush and halter her so that the befriending process could begin, while also helping to prevent possible injury to her. Arana had been in the crush a number of times since first arriving at the sanctuary, for lice treatments and worming; it allowed people to get close to her and touch her safely, and Vicki was hopeful that having gentle hands on her would help Arana realise that we weren't there to hurt her. Letting her work herself up, as she was currently doing, would only cause her to lose weight and potentially develop ulcers through stress, or hoof abscesses from constant movement on the fine gravel surface.

After opening up the gate into the crush, Vicki walked back into Arana's yard. Seeing a means of escape, the mare quickly darted into the opening of the crush and the gate was closed after her. Vicki first talked quietly to her, then reached out a hand and lightly brushed her fingers over the mare's rump. Startled, Arana half reared and then stood trembling as Vicki kept a gentle hand on her and assessed the situation. While there were usually clear benefits from a hands-on approach, she didn't want to cause the mare undue trauma. Standing above Arana in the crush, Vicki looped a rope around the mare's neck; Arana threw her head up at the initial contact but settled down gradually once it was secure, and Vicki was able to rub her over her neck, shoulders and back over the next 20 minutes. Satisfied with this progress, Vicki opened the gate and let Arana trot back into her yard.

Although the mare wasn't haltered, the rope helped. At first, Vicki kept it slack while Arana trotted around her; once she saw the mare relax slightly, she applied just the slightest pressure to the rope. Arana flicked an ear and quickly slowed, turning in to face Vicki. Although trembling and obviously tense, it was the first time the mare had stood still and Vicki slowly backed up, letting the rope go slack; the extra distance let the mare relax further. Slowly, Vicki took a step forward and then stood still, allowing the mare to relax again before continuing. Once or twice Arana went to move off, but a little squeeze on the rope was enough to keep her steady — she seemed to understand what pressure on the rope meant. Over the next 40 minutes, Vicki kept advancing and retreating, in tune with Arana's body language, until she stood beside the mare and slowly reached out to touch her. At the first contact, although brief, the flighty mare darted off, trotting around Vicki a few times before coming back to a halt. Vicki started advancing and retreating again, and this time it only took 10 minutes for her to get close. Slowly, Vicki reached out to rub Arana's neck and head. Her eye and body language had relaxed significantly, and Vicki continued to work with her slowly and steadily until she could halter her.

Once Vicki's hands were on her, Arana noticeably relaxed and pressed into Vicki's chest; the mare also licked her lips, which is a sign of both acceptance and relaxation. Soon Vicki was able to stroke and scratch her over her head, neck and shoulders while she stood still; the most at ease she'd been so far. When Vicki released her, she only paced a little bit this time. Vicki gave her some hay, making sure to put it at the furthest end of the yard as Arana was still unsure about stepping forward to eat if any people were around.

With Arana worked, I entered Shyla's yard and we repeated many of the previous day's lessons. First I got her to face me. This time, though, when I backed away to reward her the mare stepped towards me and soon she was following me around the yard, turning to copy me each time I changed directions. Amazed by her performance I left the yard to pick some fresh grass — she deserved a reward for being so willing to be with me. This time she was much braver, with no hesitation when she stepped forward and stretched out her head to take the offered grass. Feeling that Shyla was ready for more, I gently reached out a hand to touch her — and she tossed her head away before lowering it to the ground to avoid the contact. Getting to the stage of touching her was clearly going to be a slow process. I continued to work slowly with her, gradually reaching out to touch her on the shoulder. The first few times she walked away, carefully dodging me, but soon she halted in the middle of the yard, allowing my hand to touch her shoulder.

I slowly started scratching her, and rather than reacting by jumping away, Shyla lowered her head and froze. Carefully I inched closer and soon I was able to stroke her neck as well. I was impressed with her relaxed attitude but slightly concerned about her lowered head, so I backed away, crouched down and waited. The quietest wild horses are often the most easily misinterpreted; I knew how important it was to make sure that Shyla was actually mentally ready for everything I asked of her. I focused on getting her looking at me again rather than me touching her, so that when she was ready she could initiate the next contact. After a short while she stretched out her muzzle and bumped it against my hand — this was a huge milestone and I rewarded her with both my voice and a handful of hay. A few minutes later she stepped towards me again and, gradually, over the next half an hour, I was able to touch her on both her head and the left side of her neck without her lowering her head. It wasn't long before I got her haltered.

Meanwhile, Amanda was having no issues with Ballarat — the mare hadn't forgotten a thing from the day before. Amanda was able to touch her on the head again, as well as on the neck and shoulders. Rather than haltering Ballarat, Amanda simply looped a rope around her neck and taught her to lead. Although Ballarat was bold and confident, she would sometimes remember that humans were supposed to be scary and jump away, almost as if she was shocked by her own boldness. Her sassy personality was already starting to shine through, and Amanda affectionately nick-named her Brat.

CHAPTER 4

Slow and Steady

The following morning, day four, we again repeated many of the same lessons and decided that our Brumbies were ready for their first big adventure. One at a time, we led them out of the yards; first into a laneway and then, once each horse was confident turning and stopping on the lead, down the driveway to a large paddock.

Shyla was first. I was careful to keep her in a contained area until I was sure that she would remain with me. Although the whole property was fenced, and I was sure I could catch her if she got loose, it's always best to avoid unnecessary stress on the horses — we wanted this first adventure to be a positive experience so that the horses would associate their time with us as being fun. Alexa opened the gate into the driveway and we slowly inched our way past parked trucks, tractors, feed pallets and a whole assortment of scary things spilling out of a shed. Shyla was very unsure and hesitant, but she kept walking, crouched low behind me. When we turned through the second gate into the paddock she was clearly relieved, obviously glad that the scariest part was behind her. For the next half an hour we stood quietly, Shyla eventually feeling confident enough to nibble on the sparse grass.

Feeling chilled in the cold winter weather, I was about to head back to the yards when I saw Vicki leading Arana along the driveway. It was also the mare's first time out of the yards, and she danced at the end of the lead, spooking as she passed our ute and then stepping sideways as Vicki continued on. Alexa walked quietly over to join her, ready in case

Vicki needed a spare set of hands. Once they were out of sight, I opened the paddock gate to lead Shyla back to the yards. As Arana was very easily distracted, I thought it would be safer to only have one of the wild Brumbies out in the open at a time, in case they gave each other a fright and got loose. Leading Shyla back to the yards proved to be a little more challenging, though. At the paddock gate she turned the wrong way, trying to follow in the direction Vicki and Arana had gone. Applying pressure to the rope I asked for her attention, but instead of following me she edged backward and reared, still turning towards the trees. Once she settled down, I gave her time to think things over, then again asked her to turn towards the yards; this time she followed quietly.

Having put Shyla back in her yard, I watched Amanda working with Ballarat, who was now haltered and leading easily. She was ready to head out to the paddock, but we wanted to wait until Arana was also safely back in her yard. I headed off in search of the others; it had been at least 30 minutes since they had passed me on the driveway and I was hoping nothing had gone wrong. When I reached the driveway I saw Alexa, Vicki and Arana coming towards me, and moved to the side to let them pass. As soon as the flighty mare saw me she snorted and sidestepped on her lead, trotting nervously as they drew closer. The girls stopped when they reached me and I asked how it had gone. Sighing, Vicki shook her head, then glanced over at the mare who was pacing behind her at the end of the long lead, full of tension at having so many people nearby. Not wanting to keep the upset mare there any longer, Vicki said she'd fill me in once they got her back to her yard. I slowly backed away to avoid startling the mare so that they could continue to pass. All the way, Arana was tense; her mind busy, unable to relax. Alexa and I watched from the driveway as Vicki rubbed Arana's neck when they reached the yard, and unclipped the lead to set her loose. Arana immediately ran to the far fence and began pacing, not even settling when Vicki left the yard; she was upset by the fact that Amanda was leading Ballarat out into the laneway.

Ballarat quietly followed Vicki and Amanda back to where we were standing and, unlike the older mare, she stood still as we chatted. It was obvious that Vicki was concerned about Arana; it was like her brain had been fried long before we'd ever set eyes on her. Everything she did reminded us of someone walking on hot bricks. Vicki also suspected that Arana was one of the oldest horses she'd worked with; if this was so, it would make her transition to domestication even harder. When asked if she had a game plan, Vicki shrugged and said that the only thing to help a horse like that was a lot of patience; she'd spend as much time as needed to get her quiet enough to look at her teeth so that we could find out her age.

Eager to get moving, Ballarat tugged on her lead and Amanda followed, allowing the little mare to snatch a mouthful of grass in the driveway before leading her through the gate and into the paddock. She stepped through boldly, happy to explore, and Amanda let her graze a little before running around the paddock, laughing, as Ballarat trotted after her, playfully tossing her head. The mare was a cute wee thing and Amanda was thrilled with her, although still a little disappointed with her lack of height.

Before long we returned Ballarat to her yard and headed inside to warm up, happy to spend the afternoon indoors; winter in Australia was much colder than we'd thought it would be! While Alexa and I worked at various things on our laptops, Amanda settled down to work on a book she was writing. Soon bored, Vicki headed back outside to see Arana. As the wind buffeted the cabin, we quickly lost track of time — then suddenly realised that hours had passed and Vicki still hadn't returned. Worried, we headed outside to find her. When we got to Arana's yard, there was Vicki, bundled up under layers of clothing, including a beanie and gloves, sitting reading a book. Arana had finally relaxed about an hour into Vicki sitting with her, but was unsettled again by our arrival and paced restlessly, watching us warily. Stiff and cold, Vicki slowly stood up and followed us to get hay and feed for the horses so that we could settle them before nightfall.

The following day, we led Ballarat and Shyla out together, this time first exploring the paddock and then heading down to the woods and the lake behind the house. Both Brumbies were well behaved and enjoyed their adventure, and we were proud of how happily they were adjusting to their new experiences. On our return we saw Vicki sitting on the mounting block in the grass arena, holding Arana. The mare was standing still when we first caught sight of them, but as soon as Arana spotted us she began stressing, and stood shaking as we walked down the driveway, 50 metres away from her. It was incredible that just having people within sight — no matter how far away — affected the mare so much. Even people a few hundred metres away were enough to cause her stress, although she was significantly more relaxed around Vicki by then. One morning when Vicki led her out to graze in the paddock, Arana was startled by a person appearing in the distance and pulled loose, blindly bolting through two fences before she finally calmed down enough to be approached and caught. Fortunately she wasn't injured, but it was worrying that her fear of people was so ingrained that it overrode her sense of self-preservation.

Like Arana, Alexa's gelding Ranger also had a deep fear of people. Watching Alexa work with him, we wondered just what the roan Brumby had been through. He was tense, and although he had clearly been messed up by someone in the past, he tried hard. Although he was very reactive, hard to catch and genuinely terrified of having people around, Alexa was seeing some improvement. Soon she was able to touch him over much of his body — as long as no one else was nearby; like Arana, he was much more relaxed if it was just him and Alexa. While it was good that the sanctuary had been able to take him back, it was unfortunate that he'd had six months without any handling — his fear of people was now well ingrained. It would take a long time to override it with positive experiences; a few weeks of good handling when he'd first returned might have been helpful. If anything went wrong in the future, there was a good chance he would default back to his current state: for this gorgeous roan Brumby, humans were simply not to be trusted.

SIX DAYS AFTER WE'D ARRIVED IN AUSTRALIA, and on Alexa's third time working with Ranger, she felt he was ready to be backed, her aim being to sit on him for the first time. We have often found that wild horses relax much faster once they have had a rider on, especially if most of their frights have happened with someone beside them on the ground. As she'd hoped, Ranger was very good to work with — with him in a halter but bareback, Alexa was able to jump up and down beside him and then lie over him before stretching out her legs and gently running them over his rump. Staying relaxed, he stood quietly, even with Colleen and the rest of us watching from behind the fence. After about 20 minutes of backing him, Alexa sat up on Ranger for the first time and then dismounted, before repeating the process a number of times. Pleased with how relaxed he'd been, Alexa dismounted one last time and set him loose. Instead of darting off, he stayed beside her while she scratched him; it was the most relaxed he'd been to date.

Inspired by this example, Amanda and I took Shyla and Ballarat out for another adventure. In the home paddock a little way down the driveway, Colleen had set up logs, tyres and a bridge as obstacles, and we led the horses over everything. Again I was impressed by Shyla's calm and sensible nature; there wasn't much that fazed her and she was willing to try everything I asked of her. Even wearing a cover for the first time only took her minutes to get used to. I first held the cover out for her to sniff, then rubbed it along her neck before throwing it over her back. She was by far the quietest wild horse I had worked with. Ballarat was at exactly the same stage as Shyla, although she was slightly more on edge. She was bolder, braver and quicker at everything — and this meant that her reactions also tended to be more extreme. Ballarat was often distracted, and kept scaring herself when she went up to investigate something new. As both horses had made good progress we didn't want to put them back in the yards, so set them loose in the paddock so that they could enjoy a larger area and some grass to nibble on overnight.

Unlike Amanda and me, who were seeing daily progress with our horses, Vicki was on her third day of essentially doing nothing. For hours at a time, normally twice a day, she would catch Arana and lead her out to the arena, then sit on the mounting block nearby to read; even this was resulting in very little improvement. The mare still ran and paced every morning when she first saw people, cantering around her yard until she finally relaxed enough for Vicki to approach and catch her. Once caught, Arana stood quietly while Vicki brushed the mare's head, neck, shoulders and upper back, but Vicki still couldn't get close enough to her mouth to attempt to check her teeth. Arana had also started to show signs of stiffness, from spending so much time pacing. If this was due to old age, as Vicki believed, it would not be good for her physical and mental welfare to train her for the Brumby Challenge and sale by auction. In that case, Vicki was hoping that she would be able to swap Arana with a reserve Brumby.

The next day Vicki endured six more hours of bitter cold, reading through her fourth and fifth books while sitting with Arana. The day before, we'd headed to town to get supplies and Vicki had picked up a whole collection of autobiographies to pass away the time with. Arana was gradually improving and would now stand within a foot of Vicki, often lowering her head and resting a leg while she dozed; but if another person, or even a vehicle, appeared within sight she would still back up on the lead and begin pacing, flicking an ear and snorting as she trembled with fear. Each time this happened, it would take a while for her to settle down and edge close to Vicki again.

This was one of the coldest days so far, with snow falling in the hills only 30 minutes away. As it was too cold to do much, Amanda and I headed out to the paddock to catch our Brumbies and take them for a hike. Ballarat was good at being caught, but Shyla dodged me for some minutes before I was able to clip a lead on her halter. After a light grooming, we put a surcingle on each of them and led them through the woods for an hour before taking them inside the shed to stay out of the bitter wind while we fed them. Neither of us knew how Vicki was able to sit outside in the cold for endless hours. When we asked her about it, she shrugged, saying that her options were limited and that time was the only way she could see a breakthrough happening with the traumatised mare.

That afternoon, while Vicki continued to read with Arana, I worked with Shyla in the round yard. My aim was to improve her confidence about me approaching her so that she would be easier to catch in a paddock. Unclipping the rope, I turned her loose and set to work brushing her; each time I touched somewhere she wasn't sure about, she had the freedom to move away. Over the course of an hour I was eventually able to brush most of her body with her standing quietly beside me, including her girth area, legs and the right side of her body which she previously hadn't been comfortable with. Because she'd been able to move off whenever she was uncomfortable but return when she chose, I had essentially caught her many times during the session. By the end, I was able to remove her halter for the first time and catch her easily without it.

In the next paddock over, Amanda was leading Ballarat over various obstacles. Ballarat had always been happy to have her head touched, and of the three competition mares was the easiest to catch and halter. Amanda was very pleased with her little Brumby; of all the wild horses she'd trained, she was the proudest of Ballarat's progress. Something Ballarat didn't like, however, was having two people near her at once. She was very quick to react if she didn't like something, and the first time Vicki tried to approach her while Amanda was holding her, the mare got very upset and rushed backwards. As Amanda wanted to have someone holding Ballarat when she taught the mare to pick up her feet and when backing her for the first time, Vicki and Amanda kept working with her until eventually she settled down and stood still while both of them patted her at the same time.

I hadn't planned on backing Shyla early, but on our ninth day I felt she was ready. Amanda came out to watch, setting up her tripod and camera to film the entire process. When I set to work, Shyla was startled by me jumping up and down beside her. Unsettled, she moved off and it took a few minutes before she would stand again. Like most things, however, once Shyla had decided that something was okay she fully embraced it. She stood still with her ears pricked forwards (a sign of relaxation and interest) while I jumped up to lie over her back, letting her carry my weight. After repeating this a few times, I stretched my legs over Shyla's rump and rubbed my hands all over her neck and shoulders, moving around to get her used to the weight and feel of a rider. Again she didn't mind, so I dismounted, gave her a pat and repeated the process, then sat upright on her. Once again, she just stood there quietly; I sat still and enjoyed the moment, grinning. It had only been about 10 minutes since I'd first entered her yard and started working with her; she was the easiest to back of any horse, domestic or wild, that I had ever worked with.

CHAPTER 5

Baby Brumbies

To keep busy, since we only had one horse each to work and they could only mentally and physically cope with between 20 and 90 minutes of work each day, we spent the next few days befriending many of the wild yearlings and two-year-olds at the Brumby sanctuary. Some had been saved from slaughter as babies; others had been born to mares currently competing in the challenge. Two, Tilly and Quiz, were the daughters of Arana and Shyla, and we loved seeing first-hand how these younger Brumbies shared so many of their mothers' personality traits. Of all the nine youngsters we worked with, Shyla's was the most thoughtful and relaxed; Arana's foal had a decisive mistrust of people. Like her mother, Arana's foal struggled to face anything that worried her, and she would often edge sideways and panic if asked to do something new.

Over the course of a week we got each of the baby Brumbies haltered, leading, brushed all over and happy to have their feet picked up. We also had them navigating a range of obstacles: walking through swing sets, jumping over old goal-posts and leaping up on mounds of gravel on Colleen's driveway. Working with so many young horses at once was interesting; generally, we paired up with the same ones each time to consolidate our relationships with them. A couple were stroppy — more so than the older horses we were taming — and working with them was particularly interesting. We often find that youngsters born at sanctuaries or in holding yards are more challenging than totally wild ones. In this instance, the friendliest ones were the hardest to work with; they lacked respect for people, and once we began handling them they often disengaged.

It's easy to become tuned in with the body language of wild horses because they are so responsive to the subtlest of movements. These babies, however, were a little more dulled down towards people and often ignored subtle signals. They had neither the foundations that a domestic foal has nor the natural instincts of a truly wild horse, and the first few days of working with them was less rewarding than with our other Brumbies. Unlike truly wild horses, who try to process what is being asked of them and quickly become engaged, some of the babies threw tantrums over the smallest of things; we often had to laugh at how defiant they became when asked to do something new. Little Ben, approaching three years of age, had learnt to lead with us and had already been out on a number of adventures, but when asked to walk over a small log he reared, struck out with a hoof and refused to step over it. After a little persistence and patience, however, he did walk over it, and once he understood the question we had asked he was an excellent student, trotting and jumping over a course of several logs. In comparison, the first time we led Arana, Shyla and Ballarat, in turn, over a log, the mares lowered their heads slightly, processed their options and carefully stepped over it.

Following on from my first time backing Shyla in the yard, I haltered her and took her to the round yard. Jumping on her bareback, I soon had her walking and turning confidently. Satisfied that she was ready to head out into the open I dismounted, led her out to the obstacle paddock and jumped on her again. We had a relaxing walk around the paddock before I directed her to the logs, and she stepped over them without a problem, just like she had on the lead. Feeling no hesitation from Shyla, I headed to the bridge and soon we had walked over that, too. I'd been riding Shyla for about 15 minutes, and although I usually wouldn't trot on the first ride, I just felt she was ready. Heading towards the trees, I used my voice and legs to urge her on and soon we were trotting bareback.

Again she wasn't fazed, and she gently transitioned back to a walk when I asked her to.

At this stage in her training, Shyla was about two weeks ahead of Anzac, the wild Kaimanawa stallion I tamed in 2014, and Jackie, the American Mustang I tamed in 2015. While timing means nothing — and with Elder, the old Kaimanawa stallion from the 2014 muster, it had taken over 500 days to achieve the level of training and trust I had with Shyla in just the first week — it was interesting to see how the horses varied. I initially wondered whether Shyla was excelling because I'd learnt so much over the past four years and was simply a better horse trainer, but after a lot of thought I knew it was more than that; Shyla had the most beautiful soul of any horse I had ever trained, and every time I worked with her I sensed an eagerness to please. I was so thankful to Colleen for having saved her and for giving me the opportunity to work with her.

Although Amanda felt that her mare Ballarat wasn't yet ready to move on to the ridden stage, she was coming along well; her basic handling was very well established. Ballarat still took fright easily, and Amanda was avoiding any issues developing by focusing on building solid foundations. Rather than riding, Ballarat was led out on adventures, taught to be tied up both outside and under cover, and led through narrow crushes in preparation for learning to load. She had also learnt to navigate a range of obstacles and was happy to hike out to the back paddocks of the Brumby sanctuary and stand for hours while Amanda huddled on a log, contemplating life.

As with our other horses, especially the wild ones, by now it was almost instinct that told us when each horse was ready for more. During those first 10 days, however, Vicki never got that impression from Arana. Even after endless hours of sitting with her and reading, and leading her on adventures through the woods, the mare showed no sign of relaxing around people. It took 40 minutes to get her anywhere near the bridge obstacle in the paddock; rather than make a big issue of it, Vicki was satisfied when the mare got to even a metre of the bridge. She settled herself down on the bridge, letting the mare stand close by, and was rewarded the following day for her patience when Arana stepped right up and stood with her front legs on the obstacle.

Finally, on day 11, Alexa was able to help Vicki determine Arana's age. Vicki used her thumb to encourage Arana to open her mouth and Alexa was able to take photos of the Galvayne's grooves and the cups in her teeth. The outcome was disheartening; Arana certainly wasn't a young mare and was probably one of the oldest we'd ever attempted to tame. The photos were sent through to top equine dentists in both New Zealand and America, and they confirmed Vicki's suspicions: Arana was likely to be between 17 and 20 years old. This explained not only her lack of condition and her struggle to tolerate change, but also the stiffness we had started to see in her hind end. Vicki had hoped that this was due to her constant running in the yards wearing her hooves down, but at that age it was equally as likely to be wear and tear on her old joints.

Arana was one of the oldest wild horses we'd ever worked with; Major, our old Kaimanawa stallion from the 2012 muster, had been about 18 years old when he came out of the wild. It is rare for wild horses to live that long, although not unheard of. Cloud, a famous palomino Mustang from the Pryor Mountains of America was documented in the wild into his early twenties; and an old chestnut stallion in New Zealand was thought to be 27 years old when he finally died, out on the Kaimanawa ranges. While Vicki was sure that Arana's age didn't make her untameable, she didn't feel that the Australian Brumby Challenge was the right training or sale environment for her. An older Brumby, especially one we had concerns about, would need to be paired up with the right home if it was to have the best chance; not simply sold to the highest bidder at an auction.

That evening we talked over our options, deciding in the end that we needed to talk to the VBA to see if Arana could be withdrawn from competition. While this would be disappointing for Vicki, Arana's welfare had to come first. We found Colleen at the yards the next morning; and before we could voice our concerns she said that the committee had also been discussing options — and would Vicki consider swapping Arana out for a reserve? The VBA would retire Arana, giving her a safe place where she could roam with a herd long term. It was as if they had read our minds; and the solution was even better than what we'd hoped for. Of course, Vicki agreed. She and Colleen led Arana out into the laneway, and Vicki released her halter. The mare didn't hesitate — sensing freedom, she bolted forward through the gate and cantered out to the back pasture. The old mare's handling had come to an end; without a backwards glance, she joined the herd in the distance and settled down to graze. It was a really good outcome for her. As we headed back to the yards, we again wondered whether at some point during her two decades roaming in the Snowy Mountains she had been chased and lassoed by Brumby runners; it was a distinct possibility.

CHAPTER 6

Bringing in the Reserves

Being assigned a reserve Brumby proved to be no easy task. The only two mares suitable for the competition were running wild on neighbouring farmland and needed to be passively trapped in yards, similar to how the wild Brumbies are caught in the Snowy Mountains. Unlike our original Brumbies, who had had their 18 months in the sanctuary, the reserves had only been captured from the wild in the previous spring — less than eight months ago — and they had only weaned their foals a couple of weeks earlier.

We drove down with Colleen to scout out the herd. When the Brumbies saw us, hundreds of metres in the distance, the herd leader rounded up the mares and herded them away, disappearing from sight. We followed them, slowly, until we were close enough for Colleen to point out the two she'd lined up as reserves; one was a chestnut and the other a plain bay. The herd didn't remain still for long, again wheeling around to put distance between them and us. Leaving hay near the paddock gate, we left. It was the first step in the very slow process known as passive trapping; we weren't quite sure how it would work, or if and when we would actually be able to capture the horses to begin the training process!

The next day we headed down to the property early, setting up a full set of temporary stockyards and placing hay in the yards. The plan was

that the horses would enter the yards to get the hay and then the gate —
if someone happened to be around at the time — could be closed on
them. We were sceptical about whether it would work; surely, no wild
horse would enter an enclosed area when they had plenty of grass to eat.
Keeping quiet about our doubts we smiled at Colleen, secretly hoping
it wouldn't take weeks.

To us it was unfathomable that passive trapping was so effective
that hundreds of wild horses were captured this way in the Snowy
Mountains. The 12 to 20 trap sites set up each winter in Kosciuszko
National Park will catch between 40 and 70 horses most weeks. Colleen
kindly explained how it worked. Unlike here, where we'd set up the
yards in one go, the park rangers set up a bait site — laying out hay and
hollowed-out logs filled with minerals and molasses. After a few weeks
of the horses visiting the bait site, a single corner of a yard is set up.
When the horses return they are initially cautious of this new structure,
but quickly realise that it's not going to hurt them and continue to come
for the food and minerals. Over the next few weeks, the rangers add
another panel to the yard each night while laying out food; gradually,
the horses become desensitised to the fences until eventually the bait
site is fully enclosed. At this point the only access to the feed is through
a gateway in the yard, and since the horses feel so safe in the familiar
environment they step through the gate to eat — setting off a tripwire
that closes the gate and traps them inside.

Once the trap is complete the rangers check it daily, and most
mornings horses are found and removed from the yards. Sometimes
half the herd are inside the yard when the tripwire shuts the gate; at
other times just one foal. Very rarely is the whole herd captured at
once, but typically the rest will be captured over the following days. It
amazed us that the horses were reckless enough to risk their freedom
for the taste of salt and molasses, especially after watching the stress
of their fellow herd mates when they realise there is no way out of the
fence that holds them.

To keep ourselves busy while waiting for the reserves to be trapped,
Amanda, Alexa and I continued working with our Brumbies while

Vicki concentrated on the baby Brumbies. Alexa had been making good progress with Ranger and had had her first trot on him, bareback, but we had some serious concerns about his future. With the right home and a professional and sensitive trainer he had the potential to have a good life — but he had an even greater capacity to hurt someone, or even himself. Like Arana, he had no sense of self-preservation and often would jump over or go through fences if something panicked him.

Shyla's ridden work was also coming along well, with her now being ridden at the walk and the trot under saddle, but in other ways she was defiant; she often reared as her way of dealing with things that scared her. The first time we taught the Brumbies to load on a trailer, Ballarat was excellent. Shyla, too, also walked straight on. However, when we went to reload them a second time, Ballarat was again perfect but the normally relaxed Shyla spent five minutes rearing before settling down and loading as if she hadn't a care in the world. It was a bizarre reaction — I would have expected it on the initial loading, but not after she'd done it once so calmly. Leading her off the trailer, we tried again and this third time she didn't hesitate.

THREE DAYS AFTER WE'D FIRST SEEN THE reserve Brumbies, we were thrilled to hear that Colleen had passed the temporary yards on her way home and seen the horses inside, eating hay. By the time we got there the horses were long gone, however, but Colleen was confident we could round them up. The herd 'stallion' and lead mare had been chosen especially to be Judas (traitor) horses — they were familiar with the routine of the yarding system and would lead the other Brumbies into the yards when they saw us bringing hay. Things didn't quite go to plan, as this was a different property to the Brumby sanctuary the horses were used to. Three of them, including the two we wanted, headed off in another direction and jumped a fence into the next paddock rather than following the other horses into the yards. Rather than unsettle them further we called it a night. The next morning, Colleen returned and tried again, this time with success. We quickly joined her and began the sorting process, releasing the

Brumbies that weren't needed back into the pasture until only the two reserves remained.

Up close both were lovely types. The bay mare was light in condition and significantly bigger than the others we'd seen, and the chestnut was strikingly beautiful although her conformation wasn't as correct. Unlike Shyla and Arana, who had been saved after the meat buyers had taken first pick, the following year Colleen had been able to choose some of the biggest animals before the dogger dealers arrived. The bay was assigned to Vicki, but the chestnut was also taken back to the Brumby sanctuary in case another trainer needed to swap out a horse in the next couple of weeks. Trainers had 30 days to identify any unsoundness or extreme behavioural issues with their horses that would make them unsuitable for the challenge, and Colleen didn't want to repeat the trapping process if another reserve was needed.

Although the weather left much to be desired, Vicki quickly set to work, having lost 14 days of training. The rest of us holed up inside as much as possible to avoid the wind and rain. The new mare, whom Vicki soon named VBA Zali (meaning 'special') was fairly sensible, something we had first noticed in the paddock and the yards when she was being sorted. She was quite happy with Vicki nearby, and unlike Arana she stood quietly and watched, rather than running. It was a far more typical response from a wild horse, and Vicki was relieved. By the time I ventured outside, about an hour after Vicki, she was touching the mare on her neck — although each time she inched her way forward to the mare's head, Zali would toss her head away and Vicki would have to start again.

As Vicki worked with Zali, I photographed the pair of them. Flicking through the photos on my camera, I spotted something I hadn't noticed with the naked eye: white markings were evident on Zali's back. I zoomed in and had a closer look. Along most of Zali's spine a lace pattern was evident through her winter coat; I called Vicki over and pointed them out. Now that we were looking for it, it was more than obvious. Three things could have caused it: horses can be born with a white lacing, which is a rare but beautiful spider-web-like pattern that grows as the horse grows; or it can be from a spinal injury; or, as we'd seen with the American Mustangs, it can be caused by frostbite burns from prolonged exposure to snow.

Vicki always seemed to be unlucky with wild horses: four of her five competition Kaimanawas, Mustangs and Brumbies had been unsuitable for ridden work due to injuries. It gave us a sense of foreboding, but Vicki shook her head and said surely she couldn't be that unlucky. Another injured mare at this point would mean that of the six wild horses she'd been assigned over the past two years, only one — Argo — would have been sound and healthy enough to train to any great extent. As optimistic as always, Vicki returned to the mare and gradually inched closer over the course of the next hour until she was able to get a halter on her.

Pleased with Zali's attitude and the progress she'd made, we headed inside to sleep. The next day we were taking Shyla and Ballarat to Barmah National Park for a ride out in search of wild Brumbies, and Vicki would only have a short session with Zali before we left. Unlike Arana, Zali retained much of what she had learnt the day before, and soon Vicki was touching her on the head and neck and was able to clip a lead onto the halter. Gently applying pressure on the rope, Vicki began the process of teaching Zali to lead, but as soon as the mare felt pressure on her poll she reared up. Once her feet were back on the ground, Vicki gently asked her forward again; and again the mare reared, striking out. It took about 10 minutes before she stopped rearing and begrudgingly stepped towards the pressure; as soon as Vicki felt the forward momentum, she loosened off the rope and stepped back to give Zali time to mull things over. Vicki hadn't pulled back on the rope to force Zali forward, just applied a very gentle pressure; but that had been enough to trigger the extreme reaction. Vicki, who seemed to have a sixth sense for sore and damaged horses, quietly said that she hoped Zali's reaction wasn't pain-related, because she had acted like a horse with damage to its poll.

Given the white marks and the rearing, the omens weren't good; but Vicki rightly commented that rearing was a natural response of a wild horse to feeling pressured, and not necessarily a sign of pain. The best thing to do at this stage was to build trust in the mare so that she could be handled enough to be felt all over her body; then we could see first-hand if and where she was sore. Until then, it was simply a guessing game. And even if she was sore, many issues — such as the poll — could easily be resolved with some massage and skeletal work. Vicki definitely wasn't put off, although she jokingly commented that she wished she had been assigned the chestnut Brumby as her reserve instead.

CHAPTER 7

Riding in Search of Wild Horses

As we loaded the horses for the three-hour drive to Barmah National Park, this time without any of the drama of our initial practice, I second-guessed my decision to go. Was it really a good idea to take a wild Brumby, with just three rides, out in search of wild horses? The drive provided plenty of time to rethink my impromptu decision, and as with most things in life I decided to wing it. If Shyla unloaded and was settled once we got to Barmah, I would join the others on a short ride that afternoon; if that went well, I might join in on the big ride planned for the following day.

The two-day camping trip had been a spontaneous invitation from Rob, a guy we'd met a month earlier at Fieldays, the biggest agricultural event in New Zealand, when he'd been over from Australia competing in the Rural Bachelor of the Year. He'd shown us some videos of him riding out with friends among wild Brumbies, and we'd been intrigued enough to take him up on his offer of heading out to find wild horses. Some of the highlights of our lives were seeing both Kaimanawas and Mustangs in the wild, and we knew that our work with the Brumbies wouldn't be complete unless we also saw herds in their natural landscape. Originally we'd planned to borrow stock horses from Rob, but he was a few horses short so we'd decided to bring Shyla and Ballarat.

When we arrived, we were relieved to see that the camp site was right beside a huge array of stockyards; there were plenty of safe yards to keep the horses in overnight. We chose an internal yard for our Brumbies, so that no wild horses could try to hassle them overnight or entice them to jump out to reclaim their freedom. Both our mares seemed relaxed, so I saddled up; Alexa and Vicki had borrowed horses, and Amanda led Ballarat out since we were only planning on going slowly. Feeling confident, I hopped on Shyla for just her second ride in a saddle. Unlike at the Brumby sanctuary, there were no fences within sight and I was really hoping that everything would go well. The situation reminded me of a ride in Idaho with our Mustangs where we went off in search of wild horses after they'd had just 34 days of handling; back then it had seemed dauntingly soon, and now I wondered whether it was just plain stupid to take my wild Brumby out less than two weeks after she had been touched for the first time.

The ride started off well; although nervous, I was relieved that Shyla wasn't on edge from riding out with the other horses. Rob was also on a young horse, with just a week's training under saddle, and he often deviated from the path to navigate logs and bend between trees. I was more than happy to follow the others, and it wasn't until we were 20 minutes into the ride that I finally relaxed and began enjoying it. The others had picked up on how worried I'd been, and Rob jokingly said that it was good to see some colour returning to my face. Laughing, I settled into the saddle and admitted that I was concerned about Shyla trying to follow the wild horses if we found them. I didn't mention that I was also worried about falling off and losing her, as she still wasn't totally reliable to catch.

Ironically, about three minutes later Shyla dropped to the ground beneath me to roll in the mud, and I half fell and half jumped off to avoid being rolled on. I quickly urged her up so that she wouldn't damage the saddle, but instead I just gave her a fright and she leapt to her feet and cantered off before I could grab the reins. Ahead of me everyone had stopped and turned their horses to see what was happening. My worst-case scenario had come true; I went after Shyla, hoping she would return quickly. The only thought going through my mind was that at least there weren't any wild horses in sight!

My worries were for nothing, thankfully; after passing the ridden horses, Shyla circled back and waited to be caught. I was soon remounted and we continued on our ride. Rather than stressing me out, the misadventure completely relaxed me, as I was now confident that Shyla could easily be caught and I set off through the bush teaching her to trot over logs and leave the company of the other horses. A few times we all halted to let Amanda lie over Ballarat's back while we waited; she even took her first few steps bearing the weight of a rider.

We arrived back at the stockyards just as it was getting dark, settled the horses for the night and gathered around the campfire. Rob was doing a camp oven roast over the open flames and we had borrowed swags to sleep in overnight. The food, company and country music was excellent, and some of the locals joined us, talking of their plans to save their wild horses, who were also at risk of being culled. For years, the Barmah Brumbies had effectively been managed by Nature. Every seven to 10 years, the herd numbers would grow from 125 or so up to about 600, and then a severe drought would cause them to die by the hundreds, dropping the numbers back down. The starving stallions prevented their herds from moving into the river area, to avoid other stallions' territories, and the young foals, being more vulnerable, regularly died. Eventually, desperation would cause the herd to venture nearer to the river's edge and the weakened stallions would often die trying to win the right for their herds to graze in more fertile areas.

In many ways it made more sense to passively trap, or muster, the herds every year. With the current herd size of 125, only 20 to 25 horses would need to find homes each year, ensuring that the population stayed at an optimum for the amount of grazing available. If you released the older horses and only re-homed the yearlings and two-year-olds, these younger animals would not only be at the ideal age for an easy transition to domestication, but herd numbers could also be sustained at a healthy level, preventing mass starvation in drought years.

IT WAS SURPRISINGLY WARM AND COMFORTABLE SLEEPING under the stars in winter; we were all cosy inside our swags. We woke at sunrise to wild horses grazing within sight and scrambled eggs and bacon cooked in the campfire ovens. Once we were fed, we headed over to the horses to saddle up. This time 13 horses and riders, including Shyla and me, were heading out for a three-hour ride in search of the wild Brumbies. Ballarat was staying in the yards, and since we were short of a horse, Amanda disappeared in the trees with the cameras to photograph the wild horses while we rode.

The ride started well, although Shyla was very animated with so many horses around; a few times she trotted keenly off to investigate the horses in front. I made sure everyone understood that she was recently wild and barely started under saddle, to make sure that no one took off without warning me first. Shyla was striding out well, working her way forward to get near the front. The two riders ahead of me suddenly cantered off through the trees and Shyla followed; I was unable to stop her and we sped through the bush and wove headlong between trees. It was her first time cantering with a rider on and she was very unsettled, although she did come to a halt when the other riders stopped.

My heart pounding, I looked back and saw that Rob, Alexa and Vicki were well behind. Wanting to be near riders I knew, knowing that they would keep an eye on me to make sure I was safe, I circled back to join them. For the next hour I was always careful to stay near one of the three. At times we were weaving through dense bush, but although Shyla's steering still left much to be desired I didn't have to worry. Not once was I at risk of brushing my legs up against the trees: her years in the wild had made her sure-footed and clever and she always left plenty of room.

As we trotted over logs and through flooded areas, Shyla and I both gained confidence. At one point, passing a marshy swamp, we kept in time with a fox leaping through the water and reeds; a spectacular sight. When we came out into a large clearing, Vicki urged me to try a canter — this time on purpose. I was a little worried, but agreed that it was better to practise now so that we wouldn't hold anyone back during the last two hours of the ride. True to form Shyla settled into a lovely canter, her rhythm soft and quiet, before coming back to a walk. A few other riders joined us, and again Shyla cantered well. Stoked, we pushed the boundaries throughout the rest of the ride, trotting and cantering parallel to wild Brumbies moving between the densely growing trees, and jumping over fallen trees.

I'd been walking Shyla on a loose rein for about half an hour, making our way back to camp, when four Brumbies broke through the trees and galloped towards us. They were the same ones we'd seen that morning, and as they passed, within metres of us, I was careful to keep hold of Shyla. However, although alert she didn't try to follow them. A few minutes later the stockyards were in sight and we dismounted and unsaddled the horses. It had been a phenomenal experience riding with the wild horses in such an iconic landscape, and even more special to have shared the experience with Shyla, so recently a wild Brumby herself.

Amanda was keen for one last session with Ballarat before we left, so she brought her in from the yards. As on the previous day, she was soon sitting astride Ballarat; this time with Vicki leading her around the camp site. Amanda looked ridiculously big on the mare, and she kept her knees bent so that they wouldn't hang down by little Ballarat's knees. Pleased with her progress, we loaded both Brumbies and began the three-hour drive home; keen to get back quickly so that Vicki could work with Zali.

Both Shyla and Ballarat had come so far over the past two days. Not only had they loaded and travelled for the first time, but Shyla had gone from no more than 100 metres of trotting with a rider on to confidently trekking out in a group for five hours over two days. She had even learnt to canter and jump — it was the best thing for her. Ballarat had made excellent progress, too, and had a new sense of quietness and confidence about her. After just two weeks neither Brumby was reacting like a wild horse; instead, they were looking to people for guidance and companionship. It was incredibly rewarding to have them trusting us.

CHAPTER 8

Many Hands Make Light Work

We returned from Barmah to distressing news. Back home in New Zealand, one of Vicki's young showjumpers was sick and the vets hadn't been able to diagnose a specific issue; he needed round-the-clock care, and although Mum and Paula — our stable manager — were looking after him well, Vicki really felt that she needed to be there. Although we only had 10 more days in Australia before returning home with our Brumbies to continue their training there, Vicki was concerned enough to change to an earlier flight. Fortunately, we got permission from the VBA for Alexa and me to continue handling Zali once Vicki had left. Unlike the New Zealand competition, where only the assigned trainer is allowed to handle and ride each challenge horse, the VBA understood the importance of the horses getting used to many different people; especially since most will go to strangers at auction. Amanda had decided to join Vicki, as Ballarat was already at the stage where she would be ready to fly when the time came; also, her Mustang, Bragg, had finally arrived in New Zealand from America and she was keen to get home to see him again.

Over the next three days, Vicki focused on establishing the basics with Zali: leading, loading on the trailer, being brushed all over the body, being tied up and getting caught. The day before she left, Vicki washed Zali all over, hosing and sponging her with shampoo before rinsing her off; Zali objected to it quite strongly and took a while before she would stand. Although she'd only had one week of handling and was still very raw, she was well advanced compared with how most wild horses would have been, and could now cope with all of the handling requirements she needed before leaving Australia. Alexa and I simply had to repeat the things she already knew, so these would be well practised before she flew to New Zealand.

Briar, one of the other trainers in the Australian Brumby Challenge, had arrived at Colleen's place while we were in Barmah; she was staying with us for our final week while she did the initial handling on her own Brumby, Esta, to prepare her for a 10-hour drive north to Queensland. That drive — up the length of Australia — was actually going to be much longer than the three-hour flight across the Tasman Sea for our own horses, which made us laugh.

On our final day together before Vicki and Amanda flew out, we held a Volunteer Day so that the public could come and meet the Brumbies. A lot of people had been asking to meet both us and the horses we'd been taming, and rather than having the focus on us we decided to use the extra man-power to help pull down some old fencing at the Brumby sanctuary that needed replacing. The day started with us showcasing the Brumby babies we'd been handling, and we were thrilled with how well they coped with the crowds. Everyone followed us around the property as we led the youngsters out, demonstrating how important adventures are to any horse's training. We navigated obstacles that we found along the way, both man-made and natural. To finish, everyone lined up and stepped forward one at a time to pat the Brumbies; it was amazing to see how good they were with strangers. These youngsters had only had about four to seven handling sessions each, but even Arana's foal, who was notoriously timid, enjoyed the attention and really blossomed after the experience.

We spent the next few hours pulling down almost a kilometre of old fencing; what would have taken months for Colleen and her husband Dave, trying to fit it in during their spare time, took only a few hours with dozens of people pitching in to help. Vicki, Amanda, Alexa and I all worked alongside the others and were sporting many scrapes by the end of it, but it was certainly worth it — having safer paddocks for the wild Brumbies that lived at the sanctuary would be hugely beneficial, and we loved being able to give something back after Colleen and her family had been so hospitable in having us stay with them.

After a barbecue lunch, our challenge Brumbies came out, along with Alexa and Ranger. The mares were exceptional, especially considering that they had never seen so many people together at once; I was even able to ride Shyla a little and Amanda sat on Ballarat. Ranger, though, was very unsure about having so many people around, and Alexa kept him on the lead. Even that proved overwhelming, and when I walked forward to pat him he panicked, rearing right up and falling over backwards before scrambling to his feet and jumping over two fences to get away. It was distressing for Alexa after all her work with Ranger. It took her some time to catch him, but fortunately everyone was distracted by how much Shyla and Ballarat were enjoying their cuddles, and even Zali braved a few people saying hello from a distance.

Once the visitors had left, Colleen talked with us about the best outcome for Ranger. He'd been working so well; for Alexa he was now much easier to catch, and he'd progressed from being ridden bareback to trotting under saddle. Although his panic attacks were usually worse when he was being handled from the ground, in the two days leading up to the Volunteer Day he'd also panicked with Alexa sitting on him; something he'd not done before. Both incidents were triggered by people walking too close to him, causing him to spin, rear and eventually bolt after Alexa had jumped off. Because none of the fences on the property could contain him, we often had to cross many paddocks to retrieve him, and each time he was a challenge to catch. Realising that he wouldn't be safe to rehabilitate or re-home for a long time, if ever, we discussed his options. There were two: either a very kind professional, with a very gentle training approach, needed to invest a year into him; or he needed to be left unhandled in a herd situation.

Alongside those that thrive in domestication, there will always be some wild horses that have a hard time adapting to the human world.

For these horses, generally older stallions or lead mares, having their freedom stolen away is heartbreaking, and many have a limited future once they are taken from the wild, due to behavioural and soundness issues. Elder, my older grey Kaimanawa stallion from the 2014 muster is one of these. I have thought many times that it would have been so much nicer for him to have died in the mountains he loved, rather than having to spend years adjusting to a life he will never embrace. On particularly bad days, when his hooves are so bad that I have to work with him enough to catch and sedate him so that his hooves can be done, I also wonder if it might have been kinder to have let him go to slaughter directly from the muster. A quick death at the abattoir would have saved him a lot of emotional trauma. We've always striven to do right by Elder, and have given him as much patience and time as he needs. It took 500 days before I sat on him for the first time, something I only persevered with because I honestly believed that being able to go out on the farm and to the beach would give him a better quality of life — which it did. Riding Elder has always been on his terms — he tolerates a rider purely because he loves to explore the world; he is happiest cantering down the beach or out on the hills.

There is no denying that the majority of wild horses over the age of 10 years are harder to tame; while we've had success with many older horses, others have become a burden. I could have saved and trained five wild horses with the time and money that I've invested in Elder — and even now, thousands of hours and dollars later, I have a horse that only I can catch and only a very specific way. He goes lame without shoes, yet it is unsafe to do his hooves without him being sedated and laid down on the ground. He still has the capacity to hurt someone if they move suddenly around him or do something he doesn't like. While I don't regret saving Elder and genuinely love the old boy, I also understand that he's a long-term commitment as he'll never be suitable to re-home safely. Although Elder gets genuine enjoyment roaming with our retired showjumping mares and their foals, and copes with the minimal handling asked of him, there are many times when I wish he could be released back into the wild — living out his days in the

Kaimanawa Ranges would have been the best ending to Elder's story.

Unfortunately, it's nearly impossible to gauge a horse's ability to transition to domestication from observing it in a yard or paddock; often the worst-looking ones go on to become the quietest, and vice versa. After watching Arana during the 18 months after she arrived at the Brumby sanctuary, Colleen had thought her to be an open-minded horse. The mare used to round up the herd and bring them in close if people visited, before wheeling around and leading them all away, and then repeating the process. She was highly alert and would never stand still; in hindsight, Colleen could see that this was stressed behaviour. Retiring Arana had been in her best interests, and most likely the same fate would befall Ranger — while he had potential, few people have the time or the patience to invest in a troubled horse, already mistrustful from bad experiences with people, in the hope that he would make a breakthrough. In the end, the VBA decided to let Ranger roam with a herd over the coming year and then try handling him again. If he was still wary and unpredictable, he would be retired to live out his days with one of the herds.

LATER THAT EVENING, WE HEADED OUTSIDE TO practise catching and loading the horses in the dark, as they would be flying out at night. Zali was the first to load and she did it like a professional, confidently stepping inside the dark trailer with just the shed lights to guide her. Shyla surprised us; although the easiest and the most advanced of the three Brumbies, she was the only one that balked. Within a few minutes, however, she clambered on board and stood like an angel. Little Ballarat also walked straight on, although, because there were no dividers in the stock trailer, Shyla swung sideways and pushed her out; we had to reload her twice before they both stood quietly.

Early the next morning, the vet drove out to draw blood from our three Brumbies; all of them had to have a clean bill of health before they could be imported into New Zealand. Even Shyla, who was the best around strangers, was a little nervous, and the young vet — who wasn't confident around the Brumbies — started stressing and made her worse; we ended up leading her into the crush to have her blood drawn. This was easily and simply done in the confined space, and within minutes it was over; we decided to also do Ballarat and Zali in the crush to keep the procedure stress-free.

Minutes after the vet had gone, we had the horses turned loose in the paddocks and had piled into the ute, which was already laden with suitcases, to head to the airport. By mid-afternoon we'd dropped Vicki and Amanda off at the international terminal, their time in Australia had come to an end. Alexa and I were also antsy to get home, and were hoping that we could get Zali ready in time to follow the others over the ditch within the week.

After Vicki and Amanda checked in, Alexa and I went to have dinner and a short sleep at my aunty and uncle's place in Melbourne. We slept restlessly, then got up at 2 a.m. to begin the five-hour drive to the Snowy Mountains, aiming to get there by sunrise to try to spot some wild Brumbies. Alexa held her own behind the wheel for the first four hours, waking me at 6 a.m. to swap over. Just half an hour later, I noticed the fuel light come on; assuming that we'd pass an off-ramp somewhere soon, I kept driving. Some 70 kilometres later, the fuel gauge began flashing a 'no fuel' warning; I pulled over and rang up every gas station I could find within the region. Finally, I found one that was open, just 14 kilometres away, but the attendant wasn't able to deliver fuel to us. Fortunately, we convinced the attendant to ring a local farmer, who kindly came to collect us, took us to the gas station to fill up a diesel container and then returned us to our vehicle. Soon we were on the road again, carefully following Colleen's directions in search of wild horses in the Long Plain and Kiandra regions of Kosciuszko National Park. We had the morning to look for them before meeting up with Colleen to help save a truckload of Brumbies from the very first catch of the new trapping season.

CHAPTER 9

Snowy Mountain Brumbies

As we drove deeper into the Snowy Mountains, I was excited to see a few light dustings of snow. The previous week, a snowstorm had swept through and I was keen to get photos of Brumbies in the snow. Everything about the scenery reminded me of *The Silver Brumby*, one of my favourite childhood books about the wild horses that roamed this region. Just days earlier I'd begun rereading the book, and was now excitedly recognising iconic landmarks that were mentioned in the story: the Ramshead Range, Dead Horse Gap and Thredbo River were all real places; I'd never realised that!

We kept eager eyes out for wild Brumbies. Road signs warning of wild horses indicated that they could be spotted anywhere within the next 34 kilometres. The first herd we came across was easy to find; they were only metres off the road, and we pulled over and hurriedly got out to photograph them. There were six horses in total, including a few beautiful roans. A number of cars were already parked there and several people had cameras out; to our surprise, however, no one had them pointing at the Brumbies — the people were taking tourist shots of themselves in front of the landscape! Finding it hard to believe that people wouldn't be completely enthralled by the wild horses, we left them behind, crossing the road to get closer to the horses. Our approach unsettled the horses, and they turned and cantered through the tussock before disappearing over a small hill. Quietly following, we edged closer; they remained standing long enough for us to photograph them in front of a rocky tor, before turning away.

Of all the wild horses in every part of the world, the Australian Brumby, introduced to me in Elyne Mitchell's *Silver Brumby* books, had been what first inspired my love for and appreciation of wild horses. Ever since reading those books, almost two decades ago, I had dreamed of seeing horses in the wild and of taming my very own wild horse. While both of those things had come to pass many times over the years, there was something special about seeing Brumbies in the wild — like having a childhood dream come true. I wish I could have gone back in time to tell my younger self that not only would I grow up to photograph and tame wild horses, but I also would be writing my own books about our adventures. I don't think I would have believed it.

The herd we were watching was quite shy, and not wanting to disturb them we went back to the ute and continued on. As we rose in altitude, more snow covered the ground and our excitement grew. Continuing along the mountain road, we kept a good eye out for horses; when we came across a large valley in the Kiandra area, we saw about 30 in the distance, many of them greys. Parking quickly, we grabbed the cameras and layered up in preparation for hiking through the scattered snow to get close enough to the horses to photograph them. A few hundred metres away from the road we struck a swampy marsh, our boots sinking through the snow into an icy stream below. Fortunately, it was only shallow and we didn't lose our balance and drop the cameras into the water.

Since our boots had already got wet through, we continued to soldier on through the swamp, at times wading through water well over knee-deep. It took about 10 minutes to cross onto solid ground, and we were relieved that the commotion we'd made hadn't startled the horses into leaving. Ahead of us, warily watching our approach, was a striking dapple grey stallion with a large herd, and on the hill in the distance roamed three older greys with snow-white coats and dreadlocks matting their manes and tails. Above them a darker grey stallion watched us, but he quickly rounded up his mares and galloped along the horizon, disappearing from sight in a flurry of snow.

Not wanting to scare off the closest Brumbies, we settled low in the tussock to photograph them. They were a curious bunch, and gradually crept closer to us until they were only about 100 metres away. We kept still, and as they relaxed they separated into three distinct herds. The dapple grey stallion had the majority of the mares, two chestnut bachelor colts stood off to one side, and a small herd of three plain bays drifted further back, ignoring us. The grey in particular caught our attention, and for the next hour we ignored the chill settling into our bones as we photographed him and his herd.

By the time we got back to the ute, the adrenaline had worn off and we were feeling the cold. Our legs and feet were numb from having hiked through snow and swamp; desperate to warm up, we quickly got changed out of our icy clothes and cranked up the heater as we headed back the way we had come; it wasn't long before we started to feel human again.

A short way down the road we met up with Colleen and her daughter Bridie and followed them to the Long Plain gate, which was closed for winter. The trapping season had begun just a week earlier, and every morning park rangers would be coming through these gates to remove the Brumbies caught in the traps overnight. That wasn't the reason we were there, though; Thor, a Brumby stallion they'd saved the winter before had died from severe colic a month earlier. Bridie wanted his final resting place to be in the Snowy Mountains where he'd once roamed free, and Colleen had taken a snip of his tail so that he could be returned to his homeland. Together, the four of us hiked along Long Plain Road, and then Bridie hung the tail hairs in a branch to let the wind lift them and blow them across the plains, as if Thor was galloping wild for one last time.

Touched by how deeply they cared for the stallion, although he'd never been handled or even touched, Alexa and I watched from one side. There was no mistaking why Colleen had first become involved in the taming of Australia's wild horses — like us, she was emotionally invested in every horse that crossed her path. In just the few weeks we'd known her, we had gained a huge amount of respect for her empathy for the wild horses she was able to save.

On our return to the cars, Colleen pointed out an unused trap site. We were astounded. The area where the bait was laid out and the yards were constructed wasn't camouflaged in the trees or hidden from view, like we'd imagined, but in plain sight. The first trap site was only 50 metres away from the Snowy Mountains Highway, on a wide bit of gravel road that we'd mistaken for a car park. The wild horses certainly weren't tricked into entering the yards, for the imposing fences would have been impossible to miss. Although Colleen had earlier explained how the Brumbies were lulled into a false sense of security over a period of weeks, enticed by the sweet smell of molasses and salts, while the yards were gradually built up, one panel at a time, it wasn't until we saw a trap site that we truly gained an appreciation for how passive the process is. There was simply no comparison to the helicopter mustering used with both the Kaimanawas and the Mustangs.

We wondered whether the rangers had stopped using this trap site because it was so easily accessible from the road; a few weeks earlier, we'd heard that Brumby activists had shared the GPS coordinates of certain trap sites, telling people to protest against the trapping of Brumbies by dismantling the yards or releasing trapped horses. While we understood that people could be passionate about the plight of the wild horses, there was a clear lack of understanding in such actions, which bordered on vandalism. The only thing they would achieve in the long run would be a poor working relationship between those involved in the management and the saving of wild Brumbies.

We headed next for the sorting yards near the Blowering Dam, where the Brumbies caught in the traps are initially taken. About 40 Brumbies were waiting in the yards; Colleen had room for about 10 on her truck, the first of many she would be saving this winter.

The horses we saw here were all sorts of colours and sizes. The first pen held about 15 stallions, many of which were stunning types. A few were openly aggressive, causing all sorts of mischief, and we were reminded of the stallion pens we had seen during the Kaimanawa musters. Colleen pointed out two roan stallions, although it took us a while to spot them. While her trained eye was used to the vast colour difference between their winter and summer coats, to us the roans could easily have been mistaken for plain bays at this time of year. In the next pen stood about 20 adult mares, many of which were heavily pregnant or had new-born foals. Most of the horses were fairly settled, happily munching on hay and completely unaware that there were only two options available for them: being re-homed, or being slaughtered.

To make the choices easier, Colleen had already decided on the age of horse she wanted. The VBA had started a new training initiative: a Brumby Gentling Clinic where people would attend a five-day training course, tame a wild weanling or yearling and then take it home with them. At that time, they had 12 people signed up, so many of the Brumbies saved today already had homes waiting for them. With this in mind, Colleen looked over the younger Brumbies, selecting five with good conformation and natures suited to the clinic; two were still with their mothers, who were pregnant. A young colt caught her eye, even though he wasn't yet old enough to be weaned; she saved him anyway, along with his mother, who was sure to be pregnant again — it was definitely better than them going to slaughter. Nine had now been chosen, and there was space for another one or two on the truck; by saving young animals, Colleen could fit more in than if she'd saved an entire load of older mares and stallions.

The four of us had all chosen the same favourite: a stunning flaxen chestnut colt who stood out from the others due to his curious nature and his white blaze and muzzle — which was covered in molasses, a dead giveaway as to what had enticed him into the trap. He was quickly sorted into a different yard along with the younger of the two roan stallions; it would be good for them to have each other's company both on the drive back to the sanctuary and after they got there.

Bridie had been carefully watching each horse that was saved and pairing them up with names. She called the roan stallion Gundara, the flaxen one Molasses, and the smallest of the foals became Kosi (short for

Kosciuszko). Alexa and I offered a few suggestions for the rest, but they were mostly rejected; although Bridie agreed that we could name the oldest chestnut mare Mirri, after the wise friend of Bel Bel, the mother of Thowra from *The Silver Brumby*. She seemed to have a gentle way about her so the name was fitting.

CHAPTER 10

Saved from Slaughter

With the newly saved horses sorted, Alexa and I began the eight-hour drive back to the Brumby sanctuary. Colleen wouldn't be loading the Brumbies until the following morning, but we didn't want to leave Shyla, Ballarat and Zali without contact for too long. Again Alexa drove most of the way; about two hours away from home, I swapped into the driver's seat. After running out of fuel that morning, I checked the gauge and noticed that we only had a quarter of a tank, but since it was a main road I was sure we'd soon find somewhere to fill up. Bizarrely, however, the gas stations in the next two towns we drove through were closed, and it was a case of déjà vu when the red fuel light came on again. I pulled over to google where the next major town was; it was now 1 a.m. and I didn't want to be stuck on the side of the road overnight! Finally, about 150 kilometres after I'd started driving and after about 70 kilometres of stressing, we pulled into a town with a 24-hour gas station and were relieved to find it open. We'd never had so much trouble finding fuel on any of our road trips around New Zealand or America. The next time I drove anywhere in Australia, I was determined to refill as soon as the tank was half empty or carry an extra container of diesel with me. We'd driven for 16 of the past 24 hours, and I couldn't believe we'd had such bad luck twice.

We got back to stormy weather so only worked the horses lightly the following day, catching them and brushing them in the barn before turning them out in the paddock again. Zali was a little on edge; even though we were able to catch her and take her for a walk, she was tense. She barely stood to be brushed and was significantly worse on her right side — we didn't even attempt to touch her legs or girth area. She was undoubtedly more comfortable with Vicki, but we were content with how good she'd been considering that it takes a while for wild horses to trust new people.

Before it got dark we set the yards up for the new arrivals, and then headed inside to catch up on sleep; we didn't hear the truck arrive or the horses being unloaded, and woke to find 11 new wild Brumbies in the yards. They were even more beautiful than we'd remembered, and remarkably brave, watching us closely as we mucked out around them. The two stallions in particular were curious, and both edged closer and closer. After feeding out, we helped Colleen separate off the three pregnant mares. Unfortunately, the youngest colt, which we'd assumed belonged to one of the mares, was obviously not her foal and he had to be kept back in the yards to be supplement-fed. The mares, however, were ready to head out to pasture and we opened the gate; they quietly wandered through it and we followed behind them as they slowly made their way down the laneway and out to join Arana's herd in the pasture. The colts would stay in the yards until they could be gelded.

Leaving the new ones to settle in, we headed into town to get foal formula for the young orphaned Brumby. Deciding that the trip would be the perfect practice for Zali, we loaded her, Shyla and Ballarat and headed off. The return trip took three hours, and we arrived back just before the rain set in. The forecast was for a few days of horrible weather before we were due to fly out, and as Shyla and Ballarat were sufficiently advanced in their training we decided to keep dry and just work Zali. The weather was miserable, with howling winds and heavy downpours, so we took Shyla and Ballarat inside the shed each day and tied them up for a few hours with some hay. It was useful for teaching them patience in preparation for their flight, and it also allowed their coats to dry out.

Zali desperately needed to improve in her handling. She had to pass a handling test administered by the VBA and vets before she was allowed to travel by air, and she was getting worse, not better. She was hard to catch and impossible to handle — four days before we were due to fly, it took us three hours to touch the right side of her body, which she'd been fine with just a few days before. Alexa and I persisted, very patiently, although it was frustrating — we were cold and wet, and the last thing we wanted to be doing was dealing with a mare who'd decided to revert to her wild days. Not wanting to worry Vicki, who had more than enough on her mind, we kept quiet and hoped that the next day would be better. Vicki had arrived home to work alongside the vets, doing everything possible to save her young showjumper, but they weren't able to save him and he had to be put to sleep.

Unfortunately, the weather was even worse the following day — it was snowing again nearby and the wind roared through the valley — and again Zali wanted nothing to do with us. The feeling was mutual. We were, however, desperate to get home; winter in Victoria left much to be desired and we were missing our other horses. Alexa, who was training a wild Kaimanawa for the Kaimanawa Stallion Challenges, had already been away from him for three weeks, and if we had to delay the flight because Zali wasn't ready to travel I would be staying on alone so that Alexa could go back and catch up on training.

Zali naturally didn't understand how much we were missing home, and that day it took over an hour before she'd let me touch her left side, and another three hours before I could touch her on the right side. In despair, I rang Vicki and said that it was unlikely we'd have her ready to travel in time; another week or two would probably be best. Vicki was surprised, as Zali had been doing well before she'd left, but she knew that we would make the call that was in the mare's best interest. We decided to wait and see how she was the next day before making a decision.

We woke to blue skies and calmness, a novelty after days of stormy weather. Rushing outside, I headed to the pasture to see the three new mares and Arana one last time before we left; I wouldn't have time for this after today. When I got to the paddock, Arana saw me from some distance away and immediately started running, back and forth in front of the herd as the rest of the horses turned to face me. It was incredible how strong her instincts were, even though I was standing several hundred metres away. The three new mares were quietly grazing off to one side; like the wild Brumby herds we'd seen in the Snowy Mountains, they watched us curiously rather than stressing out like Arana.

Feeling exhausted just watching her, I went back to the yards to check the other wild horses, and Alexa joined me to muck out. Once again, the colts crept closer and closer to us. When Alexa left to work Zali, I held hay out for the boys and within minutes Gundara was standing in front of me and stretching his head out to eat. He was an exceptional horse, and part of me was regretting that I was heading back to New Zealand; I would have loved to have tamed this beautiful Brumby stallion. Behind him, Molasses watched quietly before finally stepping forward to eat as well — it was amazing to think that just a few days ago they had been running wild in the mountains.

In the five minutes I had spent hand-feeding the stallions, Alexa had caught Zali — and the mare was standing quietly while Alexa brushed her all the way down her left side. I quietly moved over to watch as Alexa switched sides and groomed Zali on her right side; although tense for the first few minutes, the mare stood still, and as Alexa continued to work I could see the mare's tension leaving her. Zali must have been on edge because of the poor weather; it was a huge relief to see her back at the level of training she'd been before Vicki left.

Confident that Zali would be ready to leave in just two days, we rang the vets and arranged for them to come out and tick-wash the horses, mark off their IDs, worm them and scan their microchips. The first vet arrived early, in town clothes, and tiptoed through the muddy yards to quickly complete the IDs before hopping in her car and driving the two hours back to Melbourne. A different vet was required to do the more physical work and Anne, a lovely lady with great horse sense, arrived soon afterwards to tick off all the other boxes. To our surprise, the tick wash was more of a tick spray — all our practice washing and sponging the Brumbies hadn't been needed. The horses couldn't have cared less about having a fine chemical mist dust their coats. Worming was next, and the vet was happy for us to worm the horses ourselves, under supervision so that she could mark it off as done; again, we needn't have practised having strangers opening the horses' mouths at this early stage. It was all far less complicated than we'd anticipated, and soon all three Brumbies were signed off and ready for travel.

Drawn back to the yards, I spent some more time with Gundara. Since I'd been there first-hand to see him being saved, and knew just how close he'd been to heading to slaughter, I offered to sponsor him. My birthday was in just a week's time and it was the best use of birthday money I could think off — not only saving a life but also supporting the work of the VBA. Having saved many wild horses over the years, we know just how expensive it can be. There's no money in rescuing wild horses; mentally we have always written the financial loss off as charitable work, justifying it as giving back to the horses for everything they have enabled us to do over the years and for the invaluable learning opportunities that working with the wild horses provides.

Often, it's the emotive concept of saving a horse destined for slaughter that grabs at people's heart-strings and encourages them to re-home or sponsor a wild horse; far too often, though, the support isn't there for a horse that's already been saved. Time and time again we've seen people and organisations with the means and experience to re-home and train wild horses struggle to find homes for those they've been training, even at a cheaper price than it would cost for people to take them directly from the wild themselves. Equally bad is seeing people with the time and experience to tame wild horses be limited in how many they can work with due to the financial costs involved. If the demand and the support for people to re-home horses isn't there, it is not fair on the animals for them to be stockpiled — and nor is it feasible, as can be seen with the American Mustangs. Initiatives like the Australian Brumby Challenge and the Brumby Gentling Clinics, which lead to homes for an extra 40 previously untouched horses, are allowing the VBA to save twice as many Brumbies as in previous years.

CHAPTER 11

Homeward Bound on a Cargo Plane

Twenty-four days after arriving in Australia, Alexa and I were set to leave again. Shyla, Ballarat and Zali had passed all their vet checks, their handling was at a sufficient level and we had run through checklists in our heads to ensure that we had checked everything off. Colleen was driving us to the airport with the Brumbies, and we would be boarding the cargo plane with the horses, something we were relieved about.

Initially, we'd been told that the Brumbies would have to be based at a property near Melbourne for the two days leading to export, then be loaded onto a transporter and taken to the airport by strangers. We didn't believe that this was suitable for the Brumbies and even considered driving the horses 10 hours north to Sydney where the rules were more relaxed. Fortunately, however, we'd been able to get an exemption allowing us to transport the horses to the Melbourne airport and load them ourselves. As we were flying with them, we would also be able to check on the horses throughout the flight. Without that routine, and having familiar people around the horses, there is no way that we would have considered flying the Brumbies back to New Zealand at this stage in their handling.

Managing the horses was a huge responsibility for Alexa and me, and in those final days there were many times when we wished that Vicki and Amanda hadn't gone back early. Soon the afternoon of departure was upon us. Everything was ready except our bags, which still needed to be packed, and we were literally counting down the minutes. Then, we received a call from the airline to say that the plane was arriving an hour ahead of schedule; in a flurry, we shoved clothes in suitcases, grabbed our tack boxes and everything else and hurriedly loaded it all in the ute before catching and loading the Brumbies.

Three hours later we arrived at the cargo area of the airport and signed in before unloading the horses in the dark. In the loading area, a small fenced corral on the tarmac lit by spotlights, stood the cargo box with a ramp leading up to it. Once the horses were loaded, the box would be towed to the plane and loaded on. Because Zali was the most difficult, we decided to load her first and get her safely in her stall so that we could focus on the remaining two horses. Alexa led her slowly up the ramp — she didn't even hesitate, walking into the narrow enclosure like a seasoned pro and standing quietly while she was tied up and the gate behind her shut. Next in was Ballarat and last Shyla; both were as relaxed as Zali. It was a huge relief. With nothing left to do, we loaded our gear into the front of the box and settled in for a long wait; we had allowed 90 minutes for loading the horses, in case something went wrong or they were unsure in the dark, but all three combined had taken just seven minutes.

Time passed slowly while we stayed with the horses to keep an eye on them. Travelling with wild horses after less than a month of handling wasn't something we wanted to take for granted and we remained with them until their cargo box was safely loaded on the plane. Only then did we join the pilots and the groom employed by the airline to oversee the horses' flight. Travelling in a cargo plane was a novelty, and we loved the experience. The seats were larger and more spacious than in a passenger aircraft, the bathroom was twice as big and the meals were gourmet in comparison — and you could help yourself to food and drink whenever you wanted. There were even rooms with beds for long-haul flights. No wonder Amanda hadn't complained about flying cargo when she'd flown her pony Showtym Viking to Denmark a few years earlier — it was basically like flying first-class. Even better, we had excellent access to the horses to check on them throughout the flight, and were allowed to join the pilots in the cockpit for take-off and landing, which was thrilling.

We arrived in Auckland just before sunrise and were met at the airport by Vicki and Amanda. All three Brumbies unloaded quietly and walked straight onto the horse truck, although it was their first time loading onto one; previously they had only loaded onto a stock trailer, which just had a step up rather than a ramp. They were certainly well-travelled ponies! One of the airport staff made a comment about how quiet they were; countless horses had to be drugged to fly, or to load onto transporters at the end of their trip. The staff couldn't believe that these horses had been completely untouched just a few weeks ago, especially Zali who had had just 12 days of handling. Even we were impressed with their behaviour; although we'd put plenty of time and work into preparing them for the trip, with horses nothing's a sure thing and we'd been prepared for a few issues to arise. In every way, the Brumbies had exceeded our expectations.

Although amazed by how straight-forward the horses were to handle, the airline staff were taken aback by their size, condition and appearance; I'm sure many of them wondered just what we could see in these feral-looking ponies, or why we were investing so much time and money into taming them. In some ways that's part of the beauty of working with wild horses: the transformations are often not only from wild to tame but also from poor to well-conditioned; in addition, we've always begun taming wild horses in winter, when their fluffy coats hide much of their true beauty. Working with wild horses can be likened to finding a diamond in the rough; as a trainer you have to dig deep to see their potential, and then spend endless hours polishing the horses to realise it.

Many people ask why, as professional horse trainers who compete at the top level, we bother spending time working with the wild ones — especially when (like now) we don't get to pick the horses ourselves and have no control over age, height, colour, temperament, conformation or soundness. Sometimes we wonder the same thing! But while it's not always easy, and the time invested is huge, the lessons these horses have taught us have been so worth it. And it's not necessarily so much what these horses can teach us, but rather what we can teach others by sharing their stories. If we can inspire better welfare for horses, and encourage others to produce happier and sounder animals, then I think we've done something right in life. Throughout every level of horse ownership, the level of ignorance we often see is heartbreaking — and it's the horses that have to suffer, in silence. We've learnt a lot over the years, and have come to realise that as horse owners it's our responsibility to know when our horses are hurting and to know how to get them sound and comfortable again. Horses are constantly trying to communicate with us — all we need to do is truly listen — and we're very thankful that the wild horses have given us a platform for inspiring others to look out for their horses' best interests.

We're often asked why we consider wild horses to be the best teachers: it's because, unlike domestic horses, they aren't dulled down. Every reaction is a true reaction, so that the horses become a true reflection of your ability as a trainer. If you are too hard on them or hurt them — even if only by accident — they become mistrustful. If you allow them to take the easy path every time, you develop a lazy horse with a poor work ethic; but if you constantly nag them with your hands or legs without getting a response, then you desensitise them to these aids, sentencing them to a life of kids needing whips and spurs when riding them. We take the responsibility of training young and wild horses very seriously, because we know that what they learn first they learn best. If we can set them up to seek human companionship, be bold and willing to try new things, and be soft in the mouth, responsive to the leg and able to enjoy their life, then we know we've done well. Already we were starting to see many of these attributes in our Brumbies; as we drove north, heading home, we wondered what lessons these wild horses would teach us and where their story would take us; the only thing we knew for sure is that the road ahead was bound to have some twists and turns we wouldn't see coming.

CHAPTER 12

In the Winterless North

We arrived home in the early hours of the morning and unloaded the horses at Vicki's property, settling Zali into a stable before leading Shyla and Ballarat down the hill, across the arena and down to the bottom of the property where Amanda and I base our horses. Relaxing in a yard was Bragg, Amanda's American Mustang, who had flown in just a week earlier. I glanced over at him in surprise, barely recognising him — he was tiny! In America we'd been convinced that he was 15.3 hands (which would have made him a horse rather than a pony), but seeing him again, and especially alongside the showjumpers, he looked closer to 14.2 hands. I looked sideways at Amanda and she laughed — she'd had exactly the same reaction when she'd first been reunited with him, and wasn't sure how we'd got his height so wrong. He had seemed so much bigger than our other Mustangs, and in the Wild West the winter before we'd obviously guessed wrong; we'd had no tape measure with us.

We led Ballarat and Shyla up beside Bragg, and, even though he was smaller than we'd expected, he still dwarfed the Brumbies. We had thought our Brumbies were between 13 and 14.2 hands high, but it looked like we'd been wrong again. Pulling out the measuring stick, we checked their height and were disappointed to find that Ballarat was even smaller than we'd guessed, at only 12.2 hands, and Shyla was 13.2 hands — we hadn't ridden ponies *this* small since we were seven! Even Zali, who we'd assumed was a full-height pony, was only 14.1 hands high. We felt a little confused — we'd been around horses our whole lives, and yet somehow we seemed to have wrongly estimated the height of every wild horse we'd trained offshore! Mulling it over, we came to the conclusion that it was because we'd had nothing full-sized to compare them against. In America we'd been in a Western-dominated region, where the average height of a horse was significantly lower than our own showjumpers; everything had felt big. Similarly, in Australia we'd only been exposed to Brumbies and most of these had been young, so our own had looked big in comparison.

Leading Shyla and Ballarat out to the back paddock, we released them in with my two greys, Elder and Dancer. At 15 hands high, Elder towered over his new paddock companions and I winced — we often felt big sitting on our Kaimanawas, who were small compared with our showjumpers, but Elder looked solid and impressive in stature beside our Brumbies. I glanced over at Amanda, who was also looking concerned: these Brumbies would be our biggest challenge yet, our two especially, because they were too small for adults to ride long term. We therefore had just four months to get them quiet enough for children — a big enough task for a young pony born into domestication and already started under saddle, let alone a completely wild one.

With a lot to think about, we headed inside for a sleep. The Brumbies had had a big day and, for the first time in over a month, they had a large field to roam that was surrounded by rivers and trees. Suddenly we realised that, probably out of anywhere in the world, three of the world's most well-known wild horse breeds were on the same property.

After giving them two days off, we caught the Brumbies and spent hours brushing the dirt from their coats; their hair was nearly 3 centimetres long and mud was clinging to it. To avoid us having to groom them for several hours each day they ideally needed to be put into covers, but this would risk overheating them. They'd come from near-freezing conditions to one of Northland's warmest winters;

after weeks of wearing thermals and multiple layers of clothing, we were down to shorts and T-shirts. Clipping Shyla seemed like the most practical solution for her, so I jumped on her bareback and rode her up to Vicki's stables for a wash and a clip. Like most things, she was very accepting of the new experience and stood quietly in the aisle while I held her and Paula, our stable manager, set about clipping her. There were a few times when she objected, such as when Paula reached her lower legs and girth area, and rather than make an issue of it we left it for the day and gave her a pat. We could easily finish the job in a few days' time, and there was no point in overwhelming her when she'd been so accepting.

We'd arrived back in New Zealand just in time for my birthday, and to celebrate we headed to the beach with 10 horses in tow. The truck and trailer were filled with showjumpers, along with Shyla and Bragg, and Mascot and Instigator — Vicki and Alexa's Kaimanawa stallions from the 2016 muster. Although by now they'd been out of the wild for eight weeks, the recently gelded Kaimanawa stallions had only had a few days of handling since Vicki and Alexa had returned from Australia.

Arriving at the beach, we quickly saddled the horses. It wasn't until I was doing up Shyla's girth that I realised how stupid it had been to clip a recently wild horse that had only been ridden in a saddle a handful of times. After being clipped for the first time, horses often react to having a saddle or a rider on; indeed, I felt Shyla tense. She soon relaxed, however, and I turned to lead her over to the others, assuming that she would be fine. Behind me I felt a tug on the rope; spinning around, my jaw dropped as I watched Shyla leap up in the air before landing on all fours and putting her head between her legs like a rodeo bronc. Luckily, she settled down within seconds. I felt terrible; she'd been faultless every step of the way in her training so far, and then a miscalculation on my part had given the poor animal the shock of her life. Not wanting to have a fall on my birthday, I led Shyla for the first part of the ride. Once she was leading nicely at a walk and a trot, and seemed quite comfortable with the saddle against her recently clipped coat, I carefully mounted. I was relieved that she felt solid and steady beneath me!

The ride started well. Amanda was loving her first beach ride on Bragg, even though he seemed a little amazed at so much water — beaches were definitely not the norm in the deserts of Nevada where he'd grown up. Shyla was enjoying herself, too, and when we got round to the ocean beach I took her for a canter with the showjumpers. By now she'd had about the same amount of riding as the two Kaimanawa stallions with us, but she was significantly further ahead — cantering happily down the beach in a halter on a loose rein. While Instigator and Mascot were coming along well, confidently trotting and having a few canters, the Brumbies just seemed so much easier to tame. I wasn't sure whether it was Brumbies in general, them being mares rather than battle-scarred stallions, their transition period at the Brumby sanctuary, or even the passive trapping as opposed to the helicopter mustering. Something about the Brumbies made them stand out from the rest of the wild horses we'd worked with.

While Shyla was noticeably more advanced — so much so that it was often easy to forget that she'd once been wild — both Ballarat and Zali also had something special about them. Although a little more reactive and still scared at times, they had a gentleness and sweetness about them. For the first few days in New Zealand, Zali lived on the driveway — Vicki's favourite place to put genuinely scared horses. It was the one spot on the property where the horses could be exposed to people wandering past every hour of the day, cars driving in, and horses being saddled and ridden out on the farm or down to the arena. Initially, Zali stood warily under the trees, well away from anyone, but soon her curiosity grew and she began to relax. She started to walk up to the stable entrance to watch other horses being groomed, and munch on hay off the trailer during feed time. Although we'd barely been able to catch her in Australia, within days of being home she could be caught and handled by both Vicki and 11-year-old Gaia, one of our local students; the improvement was remarkable.

Little Ballarat was also coming along well, but although she was ready for more, Amanda was very concerned about riding her because she was so small. At only four years old, her bones were still developing, and her lack of condition also meant that she didn't have the muscles needed to carry a rider with ease. Amanda spent most of her time working Ballarat from the ground; although she backed the mare a few times, she felt guilty sitting on her and would only do so for a few minutes at a time. We'd weighed her on our horse scales once we'd got home; by the international Mounted Games Regulations she was only supposed to carry a rider weighing less than 54 kilograms, and by showing standards the rider's weight had to be no more than 57 kilograms. Amanda exceeded both of these limits. Although she understood the importance of starting a wild horse well, so that it could be set up for a good future with a smaller rider, she was adamant that putting a rider who was too heavy on a weak pony was not in its best interests. Of all the wild horses Amanda had worked with, though, Ballarat was the most advanced for the time she'd spent with her, and she was very proud of the mare's progress. It was just disappointing that the size of her assigned Brumby would limit how much time Ballarat could have under saddle. If our eyes hadn't been so off in Australia, she probably would have asked to swap Ballarat out for a reserve for welfare reasons. On the mare's forms her height had been estimated at 14.1 hands, and while we'd realised she was smaller we wouldn't have guessed that she was only 12.2 hands and weighed in at just 288 kilograms.

Although bigger, Shyla initially weighed in at a similar amount, but as she gained condition she increased to 342 kilograms and could carry me quite comfortably. I didn't like to ride her bareback, though; she was safe enough but was too small and narrow — I would often lose my balance when she turned or stopped suddenly. It made me realise just how much smaller in build she was compared with Anzac, my 13.2-hand Kaimanawa stallion from the 2014 muster. Amanda also struggled to stay on tiny Ballarat bareback, but rode her that way anyway, figuring that avoiding the extra 10 kilograms that a saddle weighed would make it easier on Ballarat.

CHAPTER 13

Camp Chaos

The day after my birthday, and just four weeks since we'd first touched our Brumbies (17 days only for Vicki with Zali), our winter Showtym Camp got under way. Forty riders and their ponies arrived, and our previously quiet property became filled with the sound of laughter and the chaos of children.

Shyla was in her element. On the first day of camp, I left her for six-year-old Lucy to hold while she dried off after a bath. Shyla spent the whole time nudging Lucy for cuddles; as I watched them, I had the feeling that she was going to make the ultimate kid's pony. She was so gentle and affectionate — this was rare in a wild animal so soon after domestication, and we attributed it to the transition time the mares had been allowed. Having worked with three wild horse breeds from three different countries, each with a different management plan, it was interesting to see the similarities and differences between the horses. While in many ways New Zealand manages the wild Kaimanawa population best, Australia's way of capturing them has to be the less stressful, especially for those Brumbies that are then saved through the VBA and are given down-time with a herd while the stallions recover from gelding and the mares from foaling.

As Lucy hadn't brought a pony to camp, I paired her up with Shyla for the obstacle challenge on the arena, during which I photographed the riders attempting to lead and ride their horses through, under and over a range of obstacles. Vicki's Kaimanawa Mascot was paired up with Lucy's older brother, eight-year-old Harvey, and Vicki and I kept a careful eye on both children as they led their wild ponies, with only a month of handling, under flapping flags, got them to stand while balls were kicked around them, and had them balancing on a rocking bridge and standing on a raised box. Both Shyla and Mascot were better than most of the camp ponies and followed their little charges around as if they'd been doing it all their lives.

The camp kids loved meeting the wild horses and watching them being worked, and feeling that Shyla was ready for a ride I legged Gaia up on to her for a bareback lead around the arena. The mare was again unsettled by the feeling of a rider on her recently clipped coat; she froze before hunching her back in discomfort. Giving her a few pats, we waited for her to relax and then began leading her around the arena, first just walking and trotting, and then tackling some of the obstacles. Impressed, with her performance, we gave her another pat and Gaia dismounted before I passed her to Lucy again so that I could photograph the kids jumping in a Tip 'n' Out competition, where the jump height is raised every round to see who can jump the highest.

To finish up, Harvey hopped on Mascot for a ride on the lead, and then kept sitting on him while Vicki asked the Kaimanawa to lie down, something she'd trained him to do. Once he was on the ground she led Zali over — our neighbour Jazz had been leading her quietly through the obstacles — and a few of the kids gathered around them for a photo. It took a bit of convincing for Zali to edge up to the chatter of little kids, but gradually she gained courage and stood still long enough for a photo. Mascot, however, was completely loving the attention — deeply thankful to have had humans join his world. He'd obviously been beaten up by other stallions in the wild and had significant injuries, which meant he would probably only be suitable as a paddock mate or a lead-rein pony, so it was very fortunate that this seven-year-old stallion was gentle and safe enough for kids.

We filled the second day of camp with lessons, bush-bashing and lots of team challenges. Once things had quietened down I got Gaia to ride Shyla again, this time in a saddle. Again she behaved excellently, although green; it was a remarkable learning experience for Gaia to work with such an inexperienced pony.

On the third day of camp, Amanda got Gaia's younger sister, Shanti, working with Ballarat; she, too, was confident that our little apprentices had the timing and feel needed to assist in the Brumbies' training. By now Amanda had ridden Ballarat a few times, although never for more than 10 minutes at a time and only at a walk, and felt that the pony was ready for more. She'd been led out over the farm with a saddle on, so the transition to having Shanti riding her was very easy. All the basics, like stopping and turning, were already established, and Amanda felt that Ballarat would benefit from having a smaller rider on her. Shanti was nervous and excited in equal parts, but having worked with many young ponies already she was more than competent. The pair started off on the lead rein, walking and trotting around the arena, soon progressing to riding by themselves, following Gaia on Shyla so they didn't have to worry about direction, while Amanda instructed from the middle. It was incredible to watch these two ponies, just 34 days out of the wild, working so kindly for kids.

With camp over, Zali, who was two weeks behind in her handling, was now also at the stage where her ridden work could begin. She was relaxed around people, had been clipped all over, was wearing a cover and could be caught and led anywhere. Vicki had begun the first stages of backing her: first jumping up and down beside her, then jumping up to lie across her bareback — and Zali couldn't have cared less. Twenty days after she'd been touched for the first time, and a week after arriving in New Zealand, Vicki sat up on Zali for the first time. The pony was calm and relaxed, and they quickly progressed to walking up the stable aisle. The next day they had their first walk on the arena, navigating the bridge and learning to steer, and just a few days later Zali was out on the beach for the first time. They meandered at the back for most of the ride, then Vicki pulled the mare up halfway down the beach and dismounted, leading her the rest of the way. Zali had been very good in such open spaces with so many horses around, and Vicki wanted to keep everything fun and easy for her.

WE'D FIRST MET GAIA AND HER YOUNGER SISTER, eight-year-old Shanti, when they'd come to our property for a birthday ride eight months earlier, and we had been so impressed by their natural talent and work ethic that Vicki had offered them lessons in exchange for helping around the stables. She recognised in them so many of the attributes that we'd had as kids. We spent hours with these kindred spirits, sharing much of the knowledge we wished we'd known at their age. Over the summer the girls, who were home-schooled, could often be found at our property, mucking out or brushing horses, and it wasn't long before they were invited to join us as Showtym Scholarship riders — for intensive training sessions that we hold for talented young riders as a way of giving back to our local equestrian community. The girls would also swim the showjumpers in the river, ride various horses out over the farm or have lessons on the arena. They rode simply because they loved horses and enjoyed being around them. It was both refreshing and eye-opening — until we'd met Shanti and Gaia I don't think we had truly realised how different from the norm our own childhood had been. Seeing their way of life, which was so different to that of most kids today, really made us appreciate how rural — and how feral — we had been as kids.

While we inspired the girls with a love of showjumping, they were equally stirred by our work with the wild horses. When Shanti wanted to save and train her very own Kaimanawa from the 2016 muster, she begged her parents to let her have a weanling. Shanti couldn't bear the thought of the Kaimanawas going to slaughter and believed that she was capable of training a wild horse. After she had printed out the re-homing forms several times and left them around the house for her mum to find, her persistence paid off and we got a phone call to ask whether we thought the girls were capable. After a lot of consideration, we decided that both were indeed ready; the experience they could gain from taming a wild horse would teach them much more about timing and feel than any domestic horse could. We also offered to mentor them. They could have their Kaimanawas delivered to our stockyards and work on the initial handling alongside us so that we could keep

Amanda and Showtym Cassanova competing in the New Zealand World Cup Finals.

From left: Amanda, me and Vicki with some of our favourite showjumpers.

From the moment we laid eyes on her, Vicki's Brumby, Arana,
would pace in her yard if humans were near.

Shyla eating from my hand on our second day together.

Amanda's first time touching Ballarat, during their second handling session.

Vicki's reserve Brumby, Zali, three days into her handling.

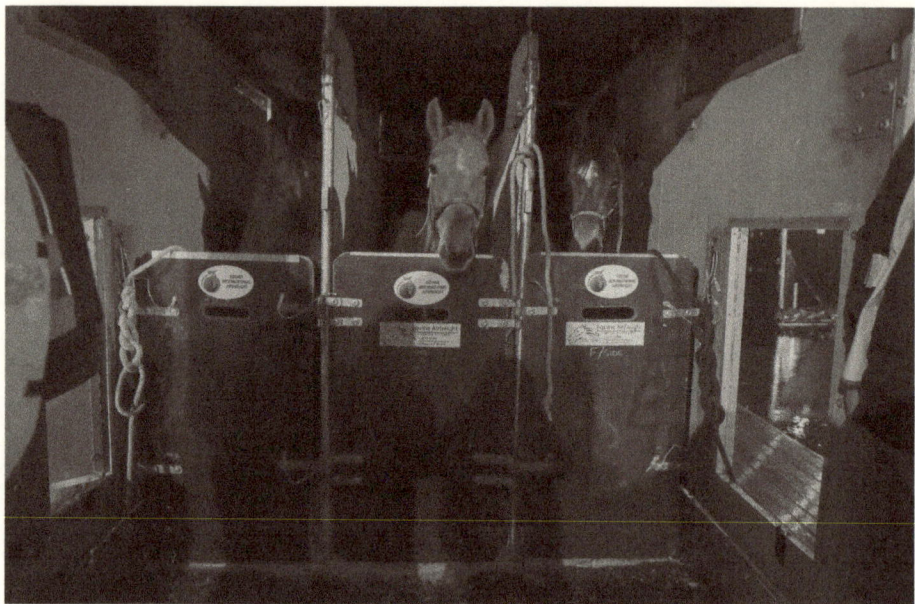

Zali, Shyla and Ballarat inside the cargo box, ready to load onto the plane to New Zealand.

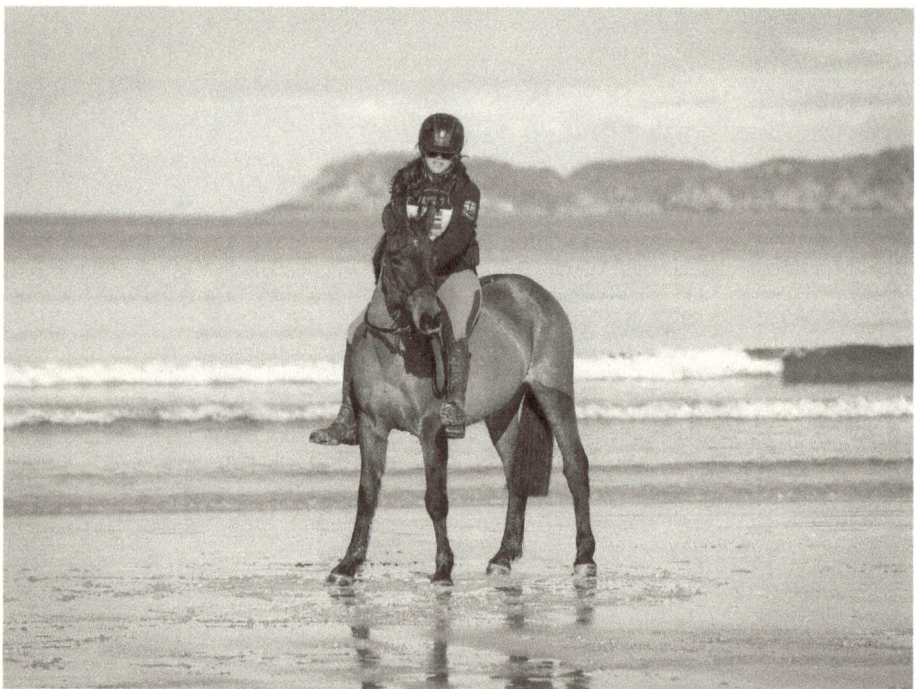

Zali 24 days from her wild state. Although she was quiet enough
to ride, Vicki only sat on her a few times due to dental and skeletal
issues which prevented her from being happily ridden.

Zali and Vicki, Shyla and me, and Ballarat and Amanda standing in front of the Australian flag after just one month of training.

A hollowed out log at an abandoned trap site, which only days earlier had been filled with molasses and minerals to trap Brumbies in the Snowy Mountains.

A herd of wild roan Brumbies near Long Plain Road in Kosciuszko National Park.

Hundreds of people marching on Parliament to protest the New South Wales government plans to cull 90% of the Brumbies in the Snowy Mountains.

10-year-old Nina's first ride on Shyla, on day 61, during our winter Showtym Camp.

Although Zali couldn't be ridden, she spent lots of quiet time
hanging out with Vicki or being led out on rides.

Shyla spending time with some of her fans during one of our Showtym Camps.

Amanda warming Ballarat up at her first training show, on day 131.

10-year-old Shanti and Ballarat jumping, a week before we left for Australia.

Shanti on Ballarat, and Nina on Shyla, enjoying a swim in the river.

Zali, 100 days after we began working with her, looking far more relaxed and significantly healthier.

Shyla and Nina cantering out over the farm.

One of our favourite wild horses, Argo, who was mustered out of the Kaimanawa Ranges of New Zealand as a stallion in 2014.

Vicki and Argo during the Battle of the Breeds at Equidays.

Amanda and Ballarat in the Ridden Pattern during the
Australian Brumby Challenge at Equitana 2016.

Shyla, with her snowflake costume, jumping during her Freestyle
class at the Australian Brumby Challenge at Equitana 2016.

10-year-old Moza with Ballarat and Amanda after placing the winning bid in the Australian Brumby Challenge auction; a dream outcome.

Shyla during the prize-giving, receiving her ribbon for placing fifth overall.

Shyla with Nina, after returning to New Zealand following
the Australian Brumby Challenge.

Moza and Ballarat competing in the Victorian State Interschool Championships
in April 2017, where they finished 10th out of 50 ponies.

Nina and Shyla at their first competition together in early 2017.

Ballarat and Amanda, Zali and Vicki, and Shyla and me; three Brumbies
that will always share a very special place in our hearts.

an eye on them and continue to teach them everything we had learnt. Then, once the horses were ready, they could go to their own property. It seemed like a win–win situation: it would allow Shanti and Gaia to have a similar experience taming wild horses as we had benefited from as children — Vicki had been nine when she'd tamed her first wild stallion (from Parekiore Mountain) and 12 when we'd tamed some wild Welsh stallions from further north — and would also ensure that two fewer horses went to slaughter during the upcoming muster without us overcommitting to too many horses ourselves.

All that was needed now was for the young girls to raise enough money; in New Zealand, saving a wild horse costs $250 for the initial purchase and more to get the horses transported up in stock-trucks, and of course there are the ongoing costs of caring for them. Determined to make it happen, Shanti and Gaia started saving money by collecting and selling manure and firewood. Then, we got an email from two passionate supporters of our work, offering to sponsor these two talented young riders to save a Kaimanawa each. We were blown away by their generosity. The re-homing application forms were due in the following week, and this offer of help would make everything financially viable for the girls. Excited about the prospect of mentoring youth with yearlings, we counted down the days until the muster, keen to see what horses they would get and what knowledge we could pass on.

When the day of the 2016 muster finally dawned, for the first time in history every Kaimanawa had a home waiting. In fact, there had been so many applications that countless people who had been approved to re-home would have to miss out; partly because a lower number of horses had been mustered than they'd anticipated. Stallions, weanlings and yearlings were in high demand, and I was one who missed out because I'd applied for a stallion but wasn't competing in the Stallion Challenges. Vicki, Amanda and Alexa were all approved trainers for the competition, and as such were guaranteed horses. Now we just had to wait to see whether Gaia and Shanti were successful and had been assigned horses.

The young girls waited on tenterhooks, ringing us every hour to see if we'd heard anything. Finally, we got a call to say that both Shanti and Gaia would get the ponies of their dreams: a wild Kaimanawa each to tame. As there weren't many weanlings, Shanti was assigned a yearling and Gaia a two-year-old filly. Being older, the horses were going to be a bigger challenge than the girls had anticipated, but we were confident that with a little help it would be all right, especially since I had no horse to tame and would be able to work with them closely.

That first day in the stockyards after the Kaimanawas had been unloaded, the girls learnt so much — as did we: trying to teach others, especially young kids, how to gently befriend a wild horse taught us a lot about our own processes. Taming has become almost instinctive for us, so trying to instruct others made us realise just how slow our movements had become, how soft and quiet our voices, and how attuned we were to the horses' body language. Many times in the early days we had to step in and show each girl how to position her body to make herself less threatening, when to wait and be patient (something very hard for young kids!) and when to ask for more. That first day I left Gaia and Shanti outside their Kaimanawas' yards while I went to watch the others interacting with the new stallions; I told the girls that the only job they had was to hold grass through the fence and talk quietly to their ponies so that the Kaimanawas would become used to both their presence and their voices. Twice the girls wandered over to watch the stallions instead; they were bored, the ponies were ignoring them and they didn't feel as if they were making any progress. Each time I took them back, talking them through the reasons why it was so important to let the ponies make the first step, and also explaining that it wasn't safe for them to be in the pens with their Kaimanawas unsupervised. Although not convinced it was working, they eventually settled against the fence, holding grass through the rails while sitting quietly and waiting. After about an hour, the ponies left their hay and wandered over to the girls, watching them curiously for a while, before eventually bending down to eat the grass from their outstretched fingers. The looks of wonder on Gaia and Shanti's faces were priceless;

it was the very beginning of a journey that would transform them as horsewomen, teaching them even more in that moment than we could have hoped for.

The timing, patience and feel both girls established over the next two months with their Kaimanawas developed in them a greater understanding of horses, both on the ground and when riding. Often when they came to train their wild horses they were joined by their two friends, 12-year-old Lily and 10-year-old Nina; like Gaia and Shanti, these two had a talent for riding and incredible attitudes to learning and we were enjoying training a growing collection of local riders. Our time spent teaching them set them up to become the perfect, size-appropriate riders to work with the Brumbies.

CHAPTER 14

The Power of Three

Having several Kaimanawas, three Brumbies and a Mustang on the property, along with our showjumpers coming into work for the competition season, gave us a lot to get our heads around. Many times we'd look back and shake our heads in disbelief at how much life had changed, and there were also many moments when we'd look forward to making plans for the future. It had only been four short years since our journey with wild horses had begun, and our lives had changed enormously through the opportunities that opened up to us along the way.

When our journey with the wild horses first started, we were, quite simply, just three young girls with a deep love of horses; three sisters who saw horses going to slaughter and believed that we could do something to help them. Never in our wildest dreams did we expect to attract the attention of publishers or television networks; or that the people in the equestrian world, let alone the general public, would be interested in our story. It's been incredibly humbling, especially when we look back at where we were as young kids: riding bareback for the lack of money to buy a saddle and only just able to afford to live week to week; there were certainly no luxuries to enjoy. There was no way we could have known where life would take us.

Four years ago, when I'd been on the brink of giving up riding to move to the city to pursue work in graphic design, I'd had no ambition to be an author and had never thought I'd be brave enough to tame wild horses. If Vicki hadn't broken her wrist, leaving me to handle the 11 Kaimanawas we saved from slaughter in 2012, life would probably have taken me away from horses, family and adventure. Before that, if Tegan Newman on Watch Me Move hadn't won Pony of the Year, or Amanda hadn't quit film school, then wild horses might not have come into our lives at all. It's even probable that if our parents could have afforded nice, well-trained ponies when we were kids, we wouldn't have developed the experience and feel needed to work with the wild ones.

I remember times when we couldn't afford to join in on school trips, had no television, wore hand-me-downs and shopped at garage sales to make ends meet. Years of living in tents and sheds because we couldn't afford to rent while we built a home, and not being able to compete in horse shows if we didn't make enough prize-money to cover our entries. Even more difficult was selling special ponies because bills needed to be paid and being shunned in the competition arena because our riding attire and saddlery wasn't on a par with that of others. Even as recently as five years ago, we would watch riders win on horses that had cost six figures and wish we could have had an opportunity like that, rather than having to search through countless horses to find the diamonds in the rough that would be competitive.

We wouldn't change a thing, though — looking back has given us an appreciation for the lessons hard won, the difficult horses we'd made breakthroughs with and the work ethic and determination that came about through years of working hard to achieve dreams that didn't come easy. Most importantly, it's given us an appreciation for each other, because without a doubt we wouldn't be where we are today without our parents encouraging us to believe that all things were possible and that we should follow our dreams, or without our own unique talents that have enabled us to be successful as individuals but even stronger when we work together.

It's amazing how, in hindsight, events make sense and fall into place when at the time you don't realise their significance. Many times over the past few years we've realised that if we hadn't met certain horses our entire lives would have been completely different. There was Just

Fine n Dandy, the very first wild stallion Vicki tamed in the winter of 1996; Sophie Bell, the very first showjumping pony that was sponsored to Vicki, who took her right through to Grand Prix level in their first season together; Showtym Girl, the very first horse to carry the Showtym name; Showtym Viking, on whom Amanda won Pony of the Year; Showtym Spotlight and Showtym Levado GNZ, whose performances with Vicki were the first to win the hearts of the public; and Watch Me Move, the Kaimanawa who changed so many misconceptions about wild horses nationwide and sparked off our own journey with them. Not to mention all the special wild ones since then: the Kaimanawas Major, Ranger, Momento, Argo, Anzac and Nikau; the Mustangs Jackie, Bragg, Rayna; and more, quite literally too many to name, but all special in their own right — and now the Brumbies.

WE WOULD OFTEN COMPARE OUR WORK WITH the Brumbies to our journeys with their New Zealand and American counterparts — not to see which one was better, because you can't judge an entire breed based on just a few animals, but because we are constantly reflecting on the lessons we have learnt and looking for where we still need to improve. Every mistake we've made along the way has been an opportunity to learn; sometimes the lessons are immediate, but often it's only with the benefit of context that we can see how far we've grown as horsewomen — especially Amanda and me, who were never the bravest of riders.

Compared with our Brumbies, our Kaimanawas from the 2016 muster hadn't progressed as far; while all three were sweet and affectionate, they were limited in how much they were physically capable of due to injuries sustained in the wild, most likely from stallion fights. Because of this, we trained the horses in areas that would specifically set them up to be successful in the coming years: Mascot spent a lot of time with kids, as he was most suited to being a lead-rein pony, while Instigator mostly trekked out over the farm as that was his happy place. Unfortunately, Amanda's Kaimanawa, Redemption, had a shoulder injury that was preventing her from starting his ridden career;

he was so sore that his body trembled if she touched the left side of his neck or shoulder. Since Redemption was generally good to handle, she felt confident that he was tame enough to turn out with other horses. Rather than pushing him past what he was capable of and causing him discomfort, she decided to forego the Kaimanawa Stallion Challenges — a year in the paddock with a herd of domestic horses would do Redemption much more good, and at only five years of age there was plenty of time to see whether he would heal.

Fortunately, we were now better at identifying and dealing with soundness issues resulting from injuries. Four years ago it would have taken us longer to find the cause of our horses' discomfort and we would have worked them anyway, wondering why we were getting problems. This time, we were able to prevent many behavioural problems from developing by only asking the horses to do what they were physically capable of.

Developing an understanding of how the equine body works and how to maintain peak soundness and happiness in our horses has probably been one of the most rewarding aspects of our work with horses over the past 20 years; especially for Vicki, who seems to have a knack for rehabilitating horses. Time and time again we see people starting horses in bits before their teeth are attended to, roping up a leg so that horses are off-balance on three legs to make it easier to back them (this too often damages their bodies), letting horses pull back while being taught to tie up (which often results in a damaged poll), putting poorly fitting saddles on horses and wondering why they buck, or riding horses that are in so much pain that their only way of coping is to rear, rush, nap or kick out. And we don't just see these things happening with young or wild horses; they also occur with far too many ponies coming through our camps and countless horses in the showjumping arena — miserable horses that are misunderstood when they try to communicate that they are in pain. By ensuring that our horses, both wild and domestic, are sound before we begin riding them, we are able to give them the best chance at a successful and enjoyable ridden career, something that is vital to us.

Knowing that prevention is better than cure, we booked the equine dentist in to do our Brumbies' teeth, and couldn't wait to have their ages confirmed and also deal with many of the dental problems that are rife in horses. A year earlier, we'd had a misunderstanding with a passionate Kaimanawa advocate because it was felt that our television show *Keeping Up With The Kaimanawas* suggested that Kaimanawas had poor teeth, reflecting badly on the breed. Argo, DOC, Elder and Hoff from the 2014 muster *did* have bad teeth, but we quickly realised that for many horse-lovers who weren't knowledgeable about equine dental care this wouldn't have seemed like the norm. Rather, it would have appeared to be an issue exclusive to the wild Kaimanawas. Nothing could be further from the truth. We have seen far too many showjumpers, young horses and bush ponies with equally severe issues. Some have never had their teeth done, while others have had work done by poorly qualified or inexperienced equine dentists.

Thankfully, the need to attend to horses' teeth is now more widely recognised; many owners get their horses' teeth done annually from a young age, preventing major issues from developing. But still, too often we get horses arriving on our property, surprisingly many coming from renowned studs and riders, with riding issues that could easily have been prevented by good dental care. One top showjumper with a rearing problem was simply reacting to fragments of blind wolf teeth that had shattered beneath her gum line, and another pony in poor condition couldn't eat properly because one of its bottom teeth had grown through into the top jaw. In many instances, sharp edges and hooks on the teeth also cause issues, by lacerating the inside of the horse's mouth. While people often believe that teeth issues are more common in older horses, many of the worst cases we have seen are in horses as young as three years of age — we try not to put a bit into a horse's mouth or expect them to work on a contact until their teeth have been looked at and treated where necessary. This is not a wild horse problem — it's simply a horse problem; the wild ones, who are often older, have just missed out on several years of potential dental care.

Our equine dentist confirmed Ballarat as being four years old, Shyla five and Zali 10. Zali's poor condition was not from having foaled at a young age, but rather, like one of our ponies several years earlier, from having a top molar missing. Because a horse's teeth never stop growing, the missing top tooth had allowed the bottom molar to grow up into the gap and then right through into the top gum and jaw. (Normally, the bottom molar would have been ground back by the top one, and vice versa.) Fortunately, our equine dentist knew how to help her; with a little time and a lot of care, he was able to correct the alignment of the teeth and surgically cut the bottom tooth back to the correct length. This explained so much about why Zali had been struggling to gain condition and why she was overly reactive to contact on her head — the locked jaw would have been incredibly painful.

CHAPTER 15

Snowstorms and Silver Brumbies

While the Brumbies recovered from having their teeth done, Alexa, Mum, Hilary (a family friend) and I headed to Australia for a Brumby protest. Wild-horse-lovers from right across Australia were marching on the New South Wales parliament to protest against the state government's plans to cull 90 per cent of the 6000 Brumbies estimated to be living in the Snowy Mountains. As well as joining the protest, we were interested in gaining more knowledge about the plight of the animals, and were keen to talk with people who were equally passionate about saving Brumbies.

A snowstorm had swept through the mountains again, and since my dream of photographing the Snowy Brumbies in deep powder hadn't really been realised, we flew over a few days early and drove to Kosciuszko National Park. This time we flew into Sydney rather than Melbourne, and the drive west was uneventful. Five hours later we arrived in Tumut, and with sunset fast approaching headed to a local pub for dinner and a few games of pool before retiring for the night.

The next morning we were awake before dawn, eager to head into the park to find the wild horses. As we drove deeper into the mountains, there was still no snow to be seen, and we wondered, with disappointment, whether it would be exactly like last time with just a little dusting of snow. But as we rounded the corner to Long Plain, we were delighted to see a white valley spread out before us, the tussock and hill slopes blanketed under a thick coating of snow. Having been obsessed with snow from a young age, I could barely contain my excitement. We drove slowly, keeping a careful eye out for wild Brumbies as we climbed higher, but within minutes a thick mist rolled in, making it impossible to see further than a few metres. Slowing the car again, we continued on to Kiandra, where we'd found the greys near the swamp, but by the time we got there we could barely see the rabbits that nibbled on the tussock alongside the road, let alone have any hope of spotting wild horses.

Stopping to photograph a falcon, we noticed hoofprints where horses had crossed over the road. Parking the car, we bundled ourselves into our snow jackets and hiked out on foot, following the trail the horses had left. The snow was far deeper than it looked; at times we would sink to our knees in the fresh powder. Remaining determined, we continued on, but soon the hoofprints faded, as if the Brumbies had disappeared like ghosts into the mist. Reaching a cascading waterfall, we paused, looked at one another and turned back; no one wanted to get lost in the never-ending white.

On our return trip to the car we found an old road, and although it was covered in a layer of snow it was easier than trudging through deep powder. Mum and Hilary spent the whole time making, then throwing, snowballs at each other, and on more than one occasion we had to duck to avoid being hit. It was fun seeing them behave like children; Alexa and I felt quite old and serious in comparison, unable to join in because we had to hold our cameras.

Having driven through the entire region that is accessible to the public during winter, we were a little disheartened to have not found a single Brumby. The lack of visibility made it both dangerous and pointless to hike out from the road to search on foot — there was a good chance we could get lost in a whiteout. Cold and wet through, we headed to the Yarrangobilly Caves to fill in time, hoping that after some food and a tour through the caves the weather would improve. The caves were located down a steep gravel road, opposite Long Plain

Road where Shyla and Zali had been trapped from, and we carefully navigated this into the valley below, leaving behind the snow and mist.

At the bottom of the valley it was hard to imagine that the weather had been so terrible higher up, and we booked in for the next possible caving tour. We had 40 minutes to wait, and to fill in time headed off in search of some nearby hot springs. The park ranger had warned us that it was a 15-minute walk each way, and with little time to spare Alexa and I sprinted down the steep track, running as if our lives depended on it. At the bottom we quickly stripped out of our thermals and snow clothes before jumping into the steaming water. As we surfaced we looked at each other in shock; the water was only tepid! Not warmed up in the slightest, we swam laps while we waited for Mum and Hilary to catch up, and then lied about the temperature to entice them to join us. As soon as they were in we leapt out, quickly towelling off before hurriedly dressing to avoid a chill.

The hike back up the hill quickly warmed us, though we only just made it back to the caves on time. Still laughing about the 'hot' pools, we fell in behind the rest of the tour group and looked carefully at the plants, rock formations and birds that the park ranger pointed out as we made our way to the cave entrance. I had only gone to the caves because Mum and Hilary wanted to, and was champing at the bit, desperate to be back up in the snow searching for horses. We only had the one day in the Snowy Mountains, and with so much snow around I knew my photos would be brilliant if only we could find horses. As soon as we entered the caves, though, all thoughts of horses left me. The caves were breathtaking: the stalactites hanging from the ceiling and the stalagmites below them looked like they were encrusted with jewels. The next hour was spent marvelling over the beauty of this underground world; it was like nothing we'd ever seen.

By the time we had driven back up to the snow level, the whiteout had cleared. Parking at the entrance of Long Plain Road, we began hiking in earnest. Because it was lower in altitude there, only scattered pockets of snow clung to the ground and we made good progress, covering several kilometres along the gravel road. Although a few kangaroos and wallabies paused for photos, no Brumbies came in sight. We'd been told that there were 12 trap sites along the first 18 kilometres of this road, though, and determined to find one we soldiered on.

Finally, we came across a muddy area containing hay, manure and an old, hollowed-out log that had clearly been filled with salt and molasses — although there were no fences, the trap site had obviously been used recently. It was just a few metres off the gravel road, surrounded by rolling plains with plenty of grass — not hidden in any way. As we walked closer to investigate, we again wondered how the wild horses could be so naïve to enter a high fenced yard and allow themselves to be caught. It had been hard to accept that they hadn't been tricked inside by the fencing being camouflaged in the bush, or that they had been so hungry that desperation made them risk everything, but seeing the trap site close up made things easier to understand. As we looked around, I wondered just how many horses had lost their freedom and their families here, and how many of them had gone to slaughter. So much tragedy had happened here; the atmosphere felt heavy, much like I imagined an abandoned city or a bloody battlefield would feel.

Having walked for almost an hour, we turned and headed back; if the trap site had been dismantled, it was probably because all the horses from this valley had either been caught or moved away to safer ground. During the long walk back, we were all quiet and reflective. Back at the car, we quickly pulled off some of our layers and were about to hop in when we saw a vehicle screech to a stop on the highway behind us. Two women, carrying cameras, jumped out and dashed up the snowy incline behind them, and our eyes searched the tree-line to see what had caught their eye. Just a few hundred metres from us, hidden among the gum trees, was a herd of Brumbies.

Grabbing our cameras in turn, Alexa and I quickly made our way towards them, slowing when we drew nearer so that the horses wouldn't take flight. A bay mare watched us with interest; behind her, a chestnut and a few roans played. Over to the side, an older, battle-scarred, roan stallion stood watch. The other two photographers quickly lost interest, but we were totally absorbed in watching the interactions between the wild horses. Hilary and Mum soon caught us up, and were equally enthralled. We found ourselves balancing on mounds of dirt, in the middle of a swamp, to get the best photos. Over the next hour we played a game of advance and retreat while the horses watched us curiously. Gradually, their courage grew and some stepped forward to investigate. The stallion and his lead mare, a striking roan who was very similar in colour, kept grazing close to the swamp's edge, keeping a careful eye on us. Taking care to keep both our boots and our cameras dry, Alexa and I headed further into the swamp, until we were crouching just 10 metres away from the herd; the horses were so close that only their heads filled the camera frame.

The experience was surreal. We have often said that, by nature, wild horses shouldn't be scared of humans. They don't fear rocks, or kangaroos, and nor do they warily avoid birds or wombats. They become cautious of things that cause them pain or fear. This herd, so similar to many of the Kaimanawas or Mustangs we'd seen in the wild, was naturally curious and interested in people; it's not until they have a negative experience that they generally engage their fight-or-flight response. Unfortunately, the process of catching a wild horse, no matter how passive, would rarely be seen as positive; the very act itself robs them of their freedom, their family and their entire way of life. However, passive trapping would have to be the least traumatising of the different mustering methods, as their first exposure to humans is when they are transported to the holding yards as opposed to being caught or chased. Many of the injuries that are sustained during helicopter musters, where horses often have to be herded for great distances, or in Brumby running, are also avoided with passive trapping, which prevents the horses from associating people with the cause of their pain. Psychologically, the horses' inability to protect themselves or avoid capture in a chase must take its toll. This would be especially so for the stallions and lead mares whose sole responsibility is to keep the herd safe.

Not wanting to interrupt the herd's grazing for too long, we slowly backed away, carefully keeping to the high ground as we made our way back over the swamp. Back at the car, we decided to head higher into the mountains for one final scout before calling it quits for the day. With the improved visibility we hoped to find horses that would have been hidden in the mist that morning.

Just a few minutes later, my eye was drawn to a man taking photographs on the side of the road and we slowed to see what he was capturing; but it was just his kids in the middle of a snow fight. As we were about to pick up speed again, I noticed movement in the trees beyond. Pulling over, we spotted a small herd of Brumbies about 200 metres away from the road, and again we hiked out to see them. This time, however, deep snow slowed our movements and we struggled through the icy drifts. Worse, the fresh powder hid a river snaking along underneath the snow, and time and time again we would fall through into the icy water, at times hip-deep in snow. A snowboard would have come in handy! As we were already wet, we powered on, ignoring the chill. Soon the horses were close enough to appreciate; the stallion was a striking silver roan and his lead mare a sooty palomino. Beyond them a few more silvers stood, as well as a beautiful grey mare who was heavily in foal. The entire herd looked like they had stepped out of the pages of *The Silver Brumby*, and we watched them in awe, not quite believing that it was real. If they'd been born in the same era as Bel Bel and Thowra, when locals could chase and lasso Brumbies as much as they wished, I'm sure that this herd would have been hunted and captured for their rare colours.

CHAPTER 16

Protests at Parliament

On our way back, we stopped at the Brumby Gate Watch camp, which was set up opposite the holding yards by Blowering Dam. Brumby Gate Watch was a group of protesters who had set up camp over the long winter to monitor the trapping of the Brumbies. A number of people were warming up around a campfire and we quickly joined them, eager to learn more about their involvement, what they hoped to achieve, and what they'd seen since positioning themselves at the gates to the holding yards at the start of the trapping season.

On introducing ourselves, we soon learnt that our reputation had preceded us, and it wasn't necessarily a good one! One of the women had recognised us from our television show and had no time for us, stating quite frankly that we were an accident waiting to happen. Another couple, however, were excited to meet us and loved the work we'd done to showcase the plight of wild horses and inspire the younger generation to love them. It wasn't the first time that *Keeping Up With The Kaimanawas* had given people a biased view of our training methods. While it was rare for the show to be seen in a negative light, the assumptions some people came to based on 130 minutes of footage could be hurtful. It's almost inevitable that this will happen — while we worked with the horses for thousands of hours over a five-month period, the demands of a reality TV show for a mainstream audience meant that the producers had to choose the most dramatic parts of the footage, and there was often no context for viewers to draw on.

After explaining our methods and having a good talk, even the woman who had initially written us off warmed up, and we began chatting about the history of Brumbies, how she saw their future playing out and why she believed that many of the Brumby groups weren't looking out for the best interests of the horses. She proposed re-introducing legal Brumby running so that locals could manage the herds in the traditional way, and refusing to re-home Brumbies trapped by the National Parks and Wildlife Service (as she believed that re-homing was essentially justifying the removal of the wild horses). Instead, she suggested that Brumby groups should intercept slaughter trucks or save Brumbies directly from the abattoirs, so that the blood remained on government hands. For a government that essentially oversees the deaths of countless Brumbies each year, it amazed me that they could honestly say that they had never been responsible for the death of a Brumby. While government employees may not be selling wild horses for meat first-hand, there is no way they could be ignorant of the fact that the dogger dealers who collect the captured Brumbies each week make their profits by delivering the animals to the slaughterhouse.

With a lot to think about, we made the long drive back to Sydney. The thing that stood out most from everything we'd seen and heard was how much difference of opinion there was between Brumby groups. While their love for the Brumbies was undeniable, everyone we'd met seemed to have vastly different ideas on what the best outcome was and how to achieve it, and they often ended up working against each other. We could only imagine what could be achieved if the Brumby-lovers could unite and work towards a common goal.

AFTER A GOOD NIGHT'S SLEEP, we were up early for the anti-government protest at the parliament buildings. Hundreds of people opposed to the government's radical plans had gathered from all across Australia, and they had a single unified aim: the near-eradication of these horses would not happen without a fight. While we waited for everyone to gather, we talked to some incredible people, including a woman who had opened up her home to foster kids and taught them how to work with horses. The kids were of various ages, but had all developed a love for horses in their new family, each being assigned a wild Brumby to work with when they first arrived. Like we'd seen with many of the kids we help at home, the horses gave them a purpose, taught them empathy and patience, and gave them something to love. Seeing how this had transformed their lives and the passion they had for the Brumbies was inspiring.

All around us people held up signs, a lovely gentleman passed out Brumby shirts, and riders on horses waited patiently for the protest to begin. Reporters photographed and filmed, people were interviewed and introductions were made. The effort that had gone into organising the protest was obvious and we felt privileged to be part of it. Shortly the procession began, and chanting filled the streets as hundreds of people made their way towards parliament; the camaraderie was powerful enough to give me chills. The desperation of these people to help the wild horses they loved was a sight to behold. As we walked, police were careful to keep traffic away from both horses and people.

For two hours, we all stood outside Parliament House while key people spoke about the cultural and historical significance of the Brumbies, the factual inaccuracies in the proposed Wild Horse Management Plan and the welfare issues that would result in ground-shooting 5400 wild horses and leaving their carcasses to rot. Not only did wild-horse advocates share their knowledge, but members of parliament also spoke out in support of the wild horses, reflecting on previous Brumby massacres and how tragically they had gone wrong. While some Brumby advocates felt that the wild horses should be managed, there was unanimous disagreement that only 600 should be left; everyone believed that this would mean the death of the Snowy Brumbies.

The High Country experiences both extreme hot burns and extreme cold snaps, which have often proved fatal to the wild herds; many people believed that reducing the wild horse numbers by 90 per cent would put the entire population at risk. In 2003 a bush fire killed 2500 of the 4000 Brumbies in the Snowy Mountains, and an extreme snow event in the 1960s wiped out most of the Brumbies in Namadgi National Park, which borders Kosciuszko. One of the biggest concerns was that under the Wild Horse Management Plan, no Brumbies would be re-introduced into any region where herds had died through natural disaster; once the Brumbies were gone, they would be supported at that management level — meaning that no Brumbies would be allowed back into the Snowy Mountains, and any seen would be culled.

As I listened to the protesters, perhaps the hardest thing for me to get my head around was their willingness to throw any other animal into the line of fire. Posters and banners, as well as speeches, focused on proposing that the government cull kangaroos, wallabies, pigs and deer instead, turning the blame for the environmental damage onto other species. The message on one banner in particular had been adapted from a popular nursery rhyme, and it left a bitter taste in my mouth:

> *This little piggy went to town on the farmer's lambs,*
> *This little piggy rooted crops and trees,*
> *This little piggy wallowed and destroyed river banks,*
> *This little piggy ate the eggs and young of our native species,*
> *And this little piggy deserves to die!*

WHILE I WOULD LOVE TO SEE THE BRUMBIES SAVED, I don't think I could justify this being at the expense of the life of other animals. National Parks and Wildlife Service aims to maintain a balance across all of the species in the protected areas, annually removing about 800 horses, 900 deer, 1800 pigs, 2000 foxes and 1300 wild dogs.

It also amazed me that so many people who were against ground-shooting or aerial culling of the wild horses could accept these as control methods for other animals. It got me thinking: what is it about wild horses that inspires people to champion their cause so strongly? In the grand scheme of things, the number of wild horses that get culled — while excessive in Australia — in no way compares to the number of domestic horses slaughtered, which again would be only a fraction of the cattle, pigs and chickens that are bred and killed each year for their meat. Why is one animal revered above another? Trophy hunting of animals is acceptable for species such as rabbits, ducks, deer, elk, moose, mountain goats and pigs, yet shooting a wild horse causes an uproar. While I was relieved that wild horses weren't allowed to be stalked and shot by hunters, it did make me wonder how people who oppose horses being killed this way can accept it for other animals, many of which are as intelligent and as prone to fear and pain as horses.

After an image of a hunter posing beside a Brumby he'd shot and killed with a bow and arrow had gone viral just a few months earlier, many pictures of slain Brumbies were posted on social media. In one, a hunter posed next to a heavily pregnant mare he'd just shot. The image caused international controversy but did nothing to stop the killing; just a week later, a father and son stumbled across a field of slain Brumbies, including a stallion and his mares. Every 10 years or so, the controversial culling of Brumbies receives attention internationally, but although there's a huge public outcry each time, nothing changes; people soon forget about the issue until it resurfaces 5, 10 or 15 years later.

As the Sydney protest came to an end we felt overwhelmed — the plight of the Brumbies was so highly controversial that we couldn't visualise a good outcome. While the Snowy Mountain Brumby population was then at a manageable number and we were confident that a sustainable solution could be found, they represented only a very small proportion of Australia's wild horse population. Who was there to act as the voice for the others, the Desert Brumbies? Was the public even aware that Desert Brumbies were gunned down from the skies by the thousands, or frequently died from starvation or dehydration during droughts because of local over-population? Equally challenging was the large number of camels that continued to roam through the same regions, or the mind-blowing number of kangaroos — about 25 million — which were protected because they were a native species (although up to 20 per cent of the population may legally be killed each year for meat by licensed kangaroo shooters).

While the number of Brumbies initially seemed daunting, a look at the size of the land mass of Australia — most of which is uninhabited — puts it into perspective. In America at the turn of the twentieth century, over 2 million wild horses roamed over a smaller area. It chilled me to imagine the trauma and mass killings endured by the wild Mustangs as that number was brought down to just 26,000 by 1971; the population has since doubled in size, even though hundreds of thousands have been caught and taken off the ranges.

It's statistics like this that make me feel relieved that New Zealand's wild horses reached just 2000 at the peak of their population and that their management over the past 20 years has resulted in a herd size of just 300 in the Kaimanawa Ranges. Only 150 need homes every two years, a tiny fraction of the horses culled in Australia over the same period.

CHAPTER 17

From Wild Brumbies to Kids' Ponies

Arriving back home to have Shyla greet me at the gate, asking for attention, was one of the most rewarding feelings I have ever had. She'd been left completely untouched while I was away, and for her to initiate contact now spoke volumes about her nature. While I'd been gone, Vicki and Amanda had made great progress with Zali and Ballarat, and I enjoyed catching up with them and seeing how the horses were coming along. Zali had relaxed hugely, and, although Vicki hadn't ridden her since her first walk on the beach, her handling was coming along well. She was now saddled and had spent the week being led around the farm and the arena by Vicki on her palomino Spotlight. Although mentally Zali was ready for more, Vicki had slowed things right down as her poll and neck had become swollen following the dental work and she was ultra-sensitive around the head area. To prevent her becoming head-shy, Vicki kept Zali's handling to a minimum, avoiding anything that would upset the mare and require her to use contact on the rope, which would in turn cause the halter to apply pressure on the swelling.

One thing Vicki was able to work on was picking up Zali's hooves in preparation for a trim. Now that the mare was confident having every inch of her legs brushed, picking up her hooves was easy and she stood calmly in the stable, with no halter or rope holding her, while

Vicki trimmed both her front and her back hooves. It was a far cry from Zali's wild antics in Australia only a month earlier when Vicki had tried touching her legs for the first time; the mare had spent more time rearing than standing on all four feet.

With Zali's head so sore, Vicki's ability to train her was essentially on hold while she healed, and Mascot, her Kaimanawa, was also showing significant structural issues that limited how much work he was capable of. Once again, Vicki wasn't having much luck with her wild horses. Luckily her focus was able to turn to her team of showjumpers. The start of the showjumping season was now only a month away and she had 10 horses gaining fitness and strength for the first show of the season, many of which were young four- and five-year-olds preparing for their first competitions.

Ballarat, though, was improving every day. When Gaia and Shanti came to stay, Shanti would work with the young mare, and Amanda was hugely impressed with how well Ballarat responded to such a small rider. For Shanti's fifth ride on her we loaded all the horses onto the truck and trailer and headed to the beach. I rode Shyla, Amanda walked beside Ballarat and Vicki was on Argo, her very special wild Kaimanawa from the 2014 muster. Alexa, Paula and some friends also joined us on an array of young showjumpers and wild horses at various stages of training.

We started by heading out along the grass verges, making our way down the quiet beach road to the estuary before walking around the point and along the ocean beach. Halfway down the beach, we came to a stop while the young horses, one at a time, first trotted and then cantered. I hopped off Shyla and let one of the young girls ride her, so that I could take some photographs. When it was Ballarat's turn, Amanda kept a close eye on her as she trotted in circles following Shyla and her rider. Feeling that Ballarat was ready for her first canter, Amanda clipped a lead rope onto her halter and ran as if her life depended on it, finally getting up enough speed that the little pony broke into her first canter; she was as relaxed as anything. After repeating the canter a few more times, Amanda set Ballarat loose, and Shanti circled her around and then cantered back up the beach towards us.

Ballarat had done remarkably well considering that it was just her fifth ride ever with a saddle and her very first canter; even more so with an eight-year-old rider rather than a professional trainer. There were very few, if any, wild horses that we would have trusted with a child so soon out of the wild, especially for such a big milestone; it was a testament to Ballarat's nature and also to the level of skill and feel that Shanti had developed while training with us over the past six months.

At home the following morning, we gave Gaia and Shanti a lesson riding the Brumbies. Even Gaia, who was about 30 centimetres shorter, 25 kilograms lighter and 15 years younger than me, looked big on Shyla. It was a huge eye-opener for us. We'd set ourselves the goal to make these ponies suitable for children by the end of their 150 days of training; initially I'd thought this was ambitious, but now, looking at the ponies, it seemed completely achievable. We realised that our sole focus now needed to be on childproofing these ponies if we wanted them to have any sort of quality of life. Because of the auction process we would have little to no control about who they would go to, so they needed to be suitable for any level of rider; most likely a younger child, because of their size. At that moment, we agreed that we wouldn't teach them anything unnecessary, like going bridleless, lying down or working at liberty (without a lead); although these were things that might win a ribbon in the freestyle final, they would not be a deciding factor in how successfully the Brumbies would transition to their new homes.

It was a bit of a shame, as Shyla was so easy and quiet that she would undoubtedly have excelled going bridleless; in fact, I'd attempted it a few days earlier. She'd been super, working with just a rope around her neck to guide her, solid as a rock as I carried the Australian flag billowing in the breeze. However, I knew that if I pursued the bridleless work I would need many sessions to perfect it for the freestyle class. I mentally crossed it off the list as unnecessary, as in the grand scheme of things it wasn't a skill she needed to know. Every minute of my time with her was far better spent establishing a solid foundation to set her up for a successful future as a kid's pony.

Watching the girls riding, from the centre of the arena, we could see plenty of room for improvement in the training of both ponies, but more importantly also their potential. How many ponies with just a month under saddle could walk, trot and canter easily with young Shanti and Gaia on them — let alone wild ones that had not been touched by humans until just six weeks previously?

Once both ponies were thoroughly warmed up, we got them working over poles laid on the ground, trotting over them while maintaining straightness and rhythm. Shyla, who'd been over her very first jump just a few days earlier with me, was brave and willing, and Ballarat followed closely behind; although a bit unsure, there wasn't any hesitation. Once they were consistently trotting over the poles, we built the fence up to a small, 30-centimetre crossbar and again the ponies came around, this time jumping it. By the end of the lesson they were happily trotting up to a 60-centimetre wall, landing in a canter and then coming back to a walk on a loose rein on the other side.

Over the next month, work continued. Winter was now in full force, and mud and rain was making riding unpleasant; the farm was too wet to ride on, so the horses were mostly being ridden on the arena or along our country roads. To prevent her going footsore, Shyla was shod and I strove to keep a balance between work and play. On some days our focus would be on walk-trot-canter transitions, learning to accept a soft touch on the reins or developing lateral work, and on others I'd ride her out in a halter and canter down the beach with the showjumpers, often giving her three or four days off between rides.

Ballarat's education had come to a halt; the glands in her neck had become swollen and she was highly sensitised and reactive. Previously anyone could have caught her, but now she began to dodge people and would leap in the air if something moved suddenly behind her. Twice Amanda had to jump off her rather than fall off when Ballarat had been startled by something. In many ways, she was completely unlike the pony we'd let the kids near just a few weeks earlier. Hoping that time off would allow Ballarat to settle, Amanda gave her a few weeks off, only catching her to change her cover or paddock.

After three weeks, Amanda began working Ballarat again. She was a classy pony, and soon, although not as quiet as she had been, she returned to ridden work, first short walks on the arena and then beach rides, trotting and cantering along the sand with Nell, a small 16-year-old who was training at our property. While fairly well used to the saddle, Ballarat was still unpredictable at times; once, at the beach, Nell dismounted to take off her hoodie and when she remounted, the pony took off quickly. Nell, who was unprepared for the sudden movement, landed behind the saddle and lost her balance, falling to the ground. Amanda spent a lot of time going over Ballarat's body, searching for reasons why she'd changed so much from her more relaxed state; feeling that the mare wasn't yet 100 per cent, she turned her out in the paddock again.

Zali, too, was getting very little work. The swelling in her head, neck and poll had worsened considerably — both the dentist and the vet were concerned that so much time had passed with absolutely no improvement, and her handling was difficult unless she was on pain-killers. The only positive was the obvious improvement in her body condition; once gaunt, with every rib showing, weeks of CopRice, hay and grass had allowed her to blossom.

Still concerned about the obvious swelling, Vicki got the dentist back six weeks after Zali's teeth had been done to check them again. Astonishingly, her perfectly re-aligned jaw had locked up again — the problem tooth having done a year's worth of growth over the past month and a half; something that is incredibly uncommon among horses. Once sedated, Zali's teeth were aligned again and then she was turned out in the hills with Argo and Spotlight, two of Vicki's friendliest horses, in the hope that time off and friendly paddock companions would allow her to heal without turning feral.

CHAPTER 18
Wild Adventure

Spring was soon upon us, and with it came a desperation to escape on an adventure. We'd initially planned to spend a few days with some friends in the Far North, riding the Brumbies out in search of the Aupouri wild horses that lived there. Unlike the Kaimanawas, these horses aren't managed, and over the years their numbers have escalated to over 1000; the largest herd of wild horses in New Zealand. The only problem was that we were short of two useful Brumbies, as they recovered, and had only Shyla to hold the fort. Deciding that the trip would be just as special if we took three different wild horse breeds, we chose Argo and Bragg to join us. Then, just a day before we were due to leave, Argo pulled up lame and Vicki loaded her palomino Spotlight onto the horse trailer instead.

Three hours later we had the horses settled in a paddock, the trailer unhitched and had headed off-road in the Aupouri Forest to look for wild horses. It didn't take long — within minutes, we found a small herd on the side of the road. Continuing on, we searched for a larger mob, and finally, in the distance, saw two herds of about 20 horses, nestled among felled pine trees. Parking the vehicles, we slowly inched our way closer and stopped on a rise overlooking the horses. A few curious ones approached and we settled down to watch them; seeing wild horses interacting with each other and observing their behaviour is one of our favourite pastimes.

With the sun low in the sky, we left the horses behind and bumped along rough sand tracks towards the beach. For the next hour, we raced along Ninety Mile Beach at low tide, searching for a quiet place to spend the night. A track off the beach looked perfect for our needs; although the crashing of the surf was bound to keep us awake and the westerly wind was probably going to give us a cold night, we loved the idea of watching the sun set over the ocean. With only a few minutes left until sunset, we parked on flat ground and quickly set up camp. We'd never owned a tent, having always slept in the horse trucks or out under the stars, and although the temperature was supposed to drop to just 1°C overnight, tonight was going to be no different.

Amanda, Vicki, Nell and Paula spread out a tarpaulin and tossed blankets and pillows on top. Alexa took the back seat of the ute with a few of our friends sleeping bunk-style in the tray, and I slept in luxury by myself in the SUV; with the seats folded down, a single mattress easily fitted in the back, so not only did I have a spacious and comfortable sleeping area but I was also out of the wind.

After setting up our beds, we walked down onto the beach below and lit a campfire to cook dinner over, while our friend Cody played his guitar. It was a great evening, spent reminiscing over the highlights from the past year and discussing our dreams for the future. We finished by roasting marshmallows over the last of the flames, then tossed sand over the embers before scaling the dunes and settling into bed. Already there was a chill in the air, and we all layered on more clothing before closing our eyes.

We woke at sunrise to the noise of waves pounding on the shore and hurriedly packed all the blankets and bedding into the back of the ute before driving off. For the next hour we navigated the rough tracks that linked the beach and forest; often we found ourselves in a tight spot and were thankful that we'd done a 4WD course several months earlier. Once everyone had had a turn behind the wheel, we headed back to the beach. We'd planned to sand-board behind the ute on old oil drums, but this proved to be far more challenging than we'd anticipated — every time we hit a shell our legs would dart out from under us. After watching Amanda and me fail time and time again, everyone else decided to boycott the idea. We then drove for almost an hour along the beach, past seals and penguins, to reach Te Paki Stream, racing through the fresh water as we made our way inland. In the deepest water, one of the guys with us tried wake-boarding behind the ute, but even there it was too shallow — nowhere near as good as wake-boarding behind the ute up the river at home, or even the time he'd wake-boarded behind Argo at the beach.

With both sand-boarding and wake-boarding counting as epic fails, we headed back to the horses, loaded them up and took them to the beach for a ride. We planned to race the horses against the Isuzus in the ultimate test of horse-power; while we had no doubt which would win, we were all keen for a good gallop along the beach. Shyla had now been out of the wild for just 10 weeks, but had improved in both strength and condition and felt confident beneath me. Vicki rode Spotlight bareback and bridleless, and Amanda fooled around with Bragg, asking him to rear on command before saddling up and following us along the firm sand to warm up. Once the horses had stretched their legs, we headed down the beach and lined up beside the ute. Cody, who was behind the wheel, gave us a false sense of accomplishment by going easy to start with; for the first few hundred metres Vicki and Amanda held their own against the ute, although Shyla quickly fell to the back, her little legs unable to keep up. Tired of teasing us, Cody put his foot to the floor and accelerated past us. Laughing, we pulled the horses up and gave them a pat, more than happy to admit defeat.

We are always careful to keep a good balance between work and play, not only for the horses but also for ourselves. Without fail, getting outside and doing something new revitalises us — and this trip was no exception. Away from technology, routine and pressure, we are able to live in the moment and remind ourselves of the most important thing about life: it's supposed to be fun. Throughout our childhood the lack of money and therefore technology meant that we sought adventures outside; rivers, waterfalls, mounds of dirt, mud puddles and swamps became our playground. Many times we would sleep out under the stars or build huts in the bush, and even now we haven't lost our love for the great outdoors and are happy to rough it.

On our way back from America the previous winter, we'd detoured to Alaska with friends to explore the last frontier. As is so often the case with us, a lack of planning and a lot of spontaneity left us stranded at the airport with no vehicles available to rent — apparently you're supposed to book months in advance in that part of the world. Our options were limited to public transport, something that would take a lot of the spontaneity out of our normal way of travelling. We took a taxi to the closest backpacker's and holed up for the night and in the morning, while walking to town, we passed a U-Haul furniture removal office. Darting inside, I asked whether they had a truck available; they did, and we settled on a price — just US$370 for an eight-day rental (down from US$880), and even better we didn't have to return it to Anchorage but could deliver it to Seward from where the next leg of our journey, a cruise to Vancouver, was leaving. This was a much better deal than the thousands it would have cost for a car and hotels, or a motorhome, and we seized the opportunity to hire the truck; it would not only provide us with transport but also give us somewhere to sleep.

Our next stop was Walmart, where we spent US$75 to buy enough blankets, pillows and foam pads for all of us. We'd done much the same thing on our great American road trip with the Mustangs that had finished just a few weeks earlier. Comfort and luxury were not our priority; our money was far better saved for adventures. The U-Haul truck was a glorified metal box, and that first night we froze. Already hours away from the only town in the area, though, we never did find a place to buy more blankets, and every night we wore layer upon layer of clothing — and even then we shivered. Surviving the discomfort was half the adventure, though, and we never considered booking into a hotel room or eating out every night at restaurants; we cooked food in tin foil over campfires, or grabbed something ready to eat from the supermarket.

Having budgeted for a regular rental vehicle, we now had money to spare. Over the next week, we took a helicopter trip, flying over glacier lakes and swooping down waterfalls before landing on a snow-covered glacier, where we mushed huskies and raced snowmobiles; it was a wonderful experience. From there we drove south, stopping at a wildlife refuge to see moose and bears, before taking a cruise around 26 glaciers in Prince William Sound and marvelling at the array of marine life we saw. Eventually we wound up in Seward and had another once-in-a-lifetime experience: hiking to a glacier, then rappelling into ice crevices and rock-climbing back out. Most of us thoroughly enjoyed it, but it was traumatising for Amanda, who was scared of heights; after we'd bullied and cajoled her in to trying a smaller crevice, she refused to attempt another. Our final adventure in the land of snow and ice was kayaking around glaciers in Bear Lake. Our timing couldn't have been better. A huge earthquake had carved huge chunks of ice off the glacier and we kayaked through the mist, awed by the floating blue, white and, at times, black icebergs that rose out of the water.

CHAPTER 19

Final Preparations

The Australian Brumby Challenge was now fast approaching, and since only one of the Brumbies had had a significant amount of ridden work; things weren't looking promising. While we personally don't put time limits on our horses' training, we were all too aware of the trainer contracts we'd signed for the challenge — we'd agreed to return our Brumbies to Australia at the designated time regardless of the level of training they'd reached, at the very least to compete in the halter class and be auctioned off. Both Vicki and Amanda were stressed at the thought of an auction, feeling that neither Zali nor Ballarat was ready for re-homing. We were in a dilemma. It would be in the best interests of the horses for them to remain in New Zealand and spend longer with us; if the competition had been based in New Zealand we would have happily showcased them, purchased them back and continued training them before matching them up with the right home later on. Unfortunately, however, the added cost of purchasing them and flying them back to New Zealand after the competition would be $7000 per horse; this level of expense was impossible to justify, especially for Zali, who wasn't even worth $500 because of her soundness issues and age.

Unlike Zali, Ballarat was suitable for re-homing, although it was important that she was matched up with the right home to ensure that her training could continue; unfortunately, with an auction there was no way to guarantee this. Ballarat needed a small, gutsy rider who was used to training young ponies. Amanda would have loved to have paired her up with Shanti to produce over the next year as a Show Hunter pony — not only would it give Ballarat a lovely home, but it would also allow her to be prepared for a lifetime of young riders. It was at times like these that we really worried over the auction process, because we knew just how important it was to pair ponies and horses up with the right homes, especially wild ones.

We often have people come to try horses who sound fantastic on the phone or look competent when riding their own horse, but this doesn't translate to a new horse — on something new, their timing and feel is off and this causes things to go wrong, resulting in a loss of confidence for the rider and giving the horse an undeserved reputation for being difficult. More common, and perhaps less well recognised, is how grass, hay and feed at a new property can affect horses' behaviour, making them spooky or highly strung. This is often why horses can undergo a complete change in personality after being purchased, but this is overlooked far too often. Another major issue is saddle fit — far too many horses develop bucking or rearing problems because of saddles that put painful pressure on their spine, either through a lack of knowledge on the rider's behalf or due to poor advice from saddle-fitters.

When a horse changes property and owners, many variables change. A horse's entire lifestyle, paddock companions and what it eats are all affected. On top of this, they go through the confusion of trying to learn new aids from their new riders. It's never an easy transition, and too often people take their new horses for granted, expecting instant results. Mum and Dad brought us up from childhood to understand that it takes six months to get used to a new horse and two years to get the best out of it. Because of this, we'd ignore them misbehaving or performing poorly, work through the issues and strive to build a partnership that would ensure in two years' time we would be able to achieve what we were aiming for. Success any earlier than that was always a bonus.

Over the years we've seen far too many good horses ruined by being sold into the wrong homes; once bitten, twice shy. Vicki once sold one of her champion Show Hunter horses, who'd been one of our favourites: a sweet, safe and easy horse who was as kind as he was successful. After passing two vet checks with flying colours, he settled into his new home well. Initially we got wonderful feedback: he was perfect to ride and they loved him. A few months later, however, we were shocked to hear — indirectly — that the new owners thought we'd sold them a dirty bucker. It was the first we'd heard of things going wrong; we tried to ring to arrange to visit the horse and find out what had happened. It was completely out of character for this horse, and we were desperate to see whether he was okay. It took some time and some convincing before we could arrange a visit, and when we got there the horse was obviously sore. A poor saddle fit wasn't helping, so we suggested that they get him seen by a vet or physio, and we also sent down the Stubben saddle we had ridden him in, to use until they could get their own.

Unfortunately he continued to worsen and, while we had no moral or legal obligation to take the horse back, we did eventually manage to do so, to ensure that he would have the care he needed. It had been almost a year since he'd been sold and months since we'd last seen him, and when he walked off the truck we were horrified. Once sweet and full of life, he was now so unsound and structurally unbalanced that he could barely walk. For the next year he rested in a paddock; it took that long before he would accept cuddles again or seek out human companionship. Unfortunately, that year saw little improvement in his soundness and we made the difficult decision to put him to sleep. An autopsy showed that he had broken part of his pelvis, which had then healed crooked. Most likely it had started as a small fracture which had then completely broken when the new owners had continued riding him; it was no wonder that he'd started bucking. The failure of the new owners to think about what might be causing his behaviour, rather than just punishing him for it, had not only cost the horse his life but had also put him through much pain and trauma.

Stories like this are why we dedicate so much of our time to understanding what makes a horse happy. If we can pick up on injuries within a day of them happening and give them time to heal, then the horses often only require a few days off, as opposed to months or years. More importantly, we can prevent a lot of discomfort and long-term damage. By taking the time to check that every horse we start and ride is pain-free, we are able to produce happy horses that love their work. This has enormous benefits — because they love their work, they do it well. Our horses have personality and character, enabling them to communicate with us. If they come out of the paddock grumpy one day, or begin refusing jumps, we begin searching for reasons. Horses don't just wake up one morning and decide to be bad; if they are doing something out of character, there's generally a reason why. The better you know your horse, the greater your ability to pick up on small issues before they become major problems.

For example, when time hadn't done much to improve Ballarat's swollen glands, we began looking at her more closely. We first checked and then treated her for ulcers, something that is common when horses have recently changed food or properties, and we checked for allergies. Immediately we noticed some improvement, and Amanda began to work with her again.

TIME WAS FAST RUNNING OUT FOR THE BRUMBIES, as we were just a few weeks off Equidays (one of the biggest equestrian events in New Zealand, with numerous competitions and clinics), and as part of that we'd been preparing a performance with our wild horses; something to showcase all three breeds. Although all three Brumbies were making an appearance, only Shyla would represent Australia in a Battle of the Breeds competition we had devised. She would compete in a series of challenges against Bragg the Mustang and Argo the Kaimanawa, and I began training her specifically for this.

The event, which was based on Mostest — one of the games we play during our camps — was designed to highlight everything the horses could do well. While all three horses didn't need to be able to do everything, at least two of them did so that there would be something for the crowds to enjoy. Most of the challenges were decided on the basis of what Argo could do. He was a favourite with the public, having won Fan Favourite in his original wild horse challenge, and since then having performed in front of thousands of people. Having the most time in domestication gave him another advantage; we figured that, like the All Blacks, it was almost a given that Argo would win on home soil. The ridden challenges for the horses included Best Canter to Halt, Best Side Pass, Best Reinback, Best Rear, Best Lay Down, Best Turn on the Haunches (or Spin) and Best Jump — these were all things that Argo could do in impressive style, needing neither a bridle nor a saddle. As Bragg could rear on command, I decided to forgo that category for Shyla and just focus on the basics. She already knew how to do most of the challenges, so it was simply a case of refining them. The only one she didn't know was the lay down, and I asked Vicki to assist me with training her.

Vicki met me at the arena and I settled in at the side, expecting a lengthy training session. To everyone's surprise, Shyla was down on the ground within a few minutes of Vicki picking up her front leg. We gave her a huge pat and a handful of feed. Over the next few days we asked her to lie down a few more times and each time she aced it, although she never really got the hang of just staying on the ground — each time, she would start rolling in sheer enjoyment. It had been 100 days since she was mustered from the wild, the same length of time we'd had to train the Mustangs for the Extreme Mustang Makeover, and I was confident that Shyla would be ready to be showcased in front of thousands of people.

CHAPTER 20

Future Focus

Following our Far North adventure, Shyla's training had changed direction. I was focusing on her future rather than the present, and there was plenty to consider. As part of the Australian Brumby Challenge, trainers are allowed to purchase their Brumbies for A$1200 — but they have to decide whether to do this a month before the competition. Otherwise, the Brumbies are entered in the auction catalogue and if trainers change their mind they then have to bid against the public. Vicki and Amanda also needed to make decisions about their Brumbies, and with both having such minimal training it was an even more difficult decision.

After selling my Mustang, Jackie, through an auction process and never meeting her new owners, I was hesitant to sell a horse this way. We'd found the auction stressful because of the unsure outcome; and because I was both proud of Shyla and quite attached to her — which is almost impossible to avoid when working with wild horses — I wanted to consider all the options so that she would have the best future possible.

Bringing her home to New Zealand after the auction would entail a cost I couldn't justify, yet I couldn't be sure of finding her the right home in Australia. With Shyla at only 13.2 hands high, I had known from the outset that she wasn't suited to be ridden long term by me, and so every aspect of her training was aimed at having a child own her. Because of this, Shanti and Gaia's friend Nina had ridden Shyla quite a few times to make sure that she was ready for a little human to love her.

Seeing Nina on Shyla just felt right; there was something about them as a duo that seemed to click. Nina had a lovely position, soft hands and a love for horses that reminded me of myself growing up. Even more importantly, Shyla loved Nina; each time the girl went out to the paddock to catch Shyla, the mare would meet her at the gate, nickering. Nina could saddle her up by herself and would ride Shyla out to the arena for a lesson; they also enjoyed lots of adventures, swimming in the river and playing in the bush.

I suddenly wondered about the feasibility of bringing Shyla back to New Zealand for Nina to ride (since I was too old to compete ponies), while also showcasing her as an ambassador for the Brumbies. Vicki and I talked with Nina's parents, to see whether they would be interested in this idea, and luckily they were. While they could certainly have chosen a pony that was far more experienced than a recently wild and still green Brumby, Vicki and I were sure that Shyla was the right fit for Nina's second pony. You don't make great riders by buying them ponies that are effectively schoolmasters — the lessons that Nina would learn from producing a pony like Shyla would be irreplaceable. Nina had been part of Shyla's journey since the mare had arrived at our property, first helping me handle her and then riding her, and the improvement we'd seen in Nina's riding was already obvious. Like Gaia and Shanti, working with a wild pony under supervision had enhanced Nina's timing and feel, as well as her patience and understanding of a horse's fight-or-flight response. It had also sparked in her a love of wild horses and horsemanship, which would stand her in good stead growing up.

Nina's parents agreed that working with Shyla would bring many benefits. They talked it over with Nina, who now had two weeks left to decide; if she felt that Shyla was the right pony, then they would help pay for Shyla to fly back to New Zealand after the competition. The agreement was that we'd share her. I would use her for demonstrations, and in between I'd mentor Nina. We'd get Shyla out competing in the Show Hunter ring and continue her transformation into the ultimate kid's pony.

Nina was incredibly excited when she heard the plan, and we set about testing Shyla in a range of situations that would both set her up to compete in the Brumby Challenge and also give Nina a chance to see whether Shyla was indeed suitable for her. To start with, we saddled Shyla up for another lesson on the arena. Nina had previously jumped her, but only following while I'd run ahead; this time, I got them working independently, trotting around a small course. Shyla was a little confused at first, looking at me and clearly wondering why I was standing in the middle of the ring, but she soon got the hang of it and jumped around a course set at 65 cm. It was only her fifth time jumping and she was starting to show very good form.

The next milestone was Shyla's first show, a local Show Hunter day to which we took several horses. I entered her in the 55-cm and 65-cm jumping classes and spent the morning plaiting her mane, then saddled up and rode out to the practice arena. She was quiet and relaxed, and she happily trotted and cantered, then jumped over the warm-up fences on a loose rein. Pleased, I rode her to the gate and waited for our turn to compete. When it was time for us to enter the ring, Shyla felt hesitant, unsure about leaving the other horses. Although she was rarely spooked, the white, grey and brown jumps, which were decorated with flowers, were also making her hesitant, so I rode her up to each jump so that she could have a closer look.

Once she'd had a look at the jumps Shyla noticeably relaxed, although she remained distracted by the horses waiting near the gate. We approached the first jump at a trot; she hesitated on take-off, then cleared it, and did the same for most of the other jumps. When we reached the far end of the ring, Shyla froze and looked around, realising that she was very much alone, and tried to turn and head back to the gate. It took a lot of encouragement to get her to take a step in a different direction, but she was soon cantering again and relaxed as we approached the last two fences — which she jumped beautifully.

I gave Shyla a huge pat and we left the arena. Nina, who'd been waiting at the gate on her own pony, Maybeline (who was just 11 hands high), gave me a smile and a quick thumbs-up before she rode into the ring on Maybeline and won the class. I was pleased that Nina could see through Shyla's poor behaviour and recognise it for the confusion it was. When Shyla and I returned to the ring for a second and then a third time, she significantly improved each time and finished by cantering confidently around most of the course.

Shyla returned from her show experience better than ever. While previously she would only trot into fences, now she was confident cantering and was really starting to show some talent. This boded well; Nina was very successful with her current pony, and if Shyla showed the capability to jump in Category B Show Hunter classes then she would be great for Nina.

A few days later, we took our showjumpers to a local cross-country course so that they could practise before competing just a few weeks later in the Derby at Equidays. I took a showjumper and Shyla, Vicki had two horses as well, and Paula rode Ngahiwi Showtym Premier, Vicki's World Cup showjumper. Our horses normally jump coloured poles, so it was very important that that they got to practise over banks and rustic obstacles before the Equidays Derby. The jumps on the cross-country course ranged from small logs right through to Open-level jumps set at 1.05 metres. As I'd only ridden the showjumper a few times, I started off by warming her up slowly and then jumping her around the smaller options. Soon I swapped onto Shyla, and that's when the real fun began. We started by trotting into small logs and quickly progressed, cantering into the bigger fences. Before long, Shyla was following the Grand Prix and World Cup showjumpers over many of the biggest fences and bravely soaring over the training jumps. At the water jump she leapt straight in — many of the showjumpers had instead spooked at the water lilies floating on the surface of the water. She was such a brave little pony; with each jump both Vicki and I were blown away by how much heart she showed, and also her scope and talent over the fences. If Nina decided to compete Shyla she would certainly have a lot of fun with her, and Shyla would be more than capable of everything Nina wanted to do.

SHYLA HAD A FEW DAYS OFF TO RECOVER from her big jumping while we were all down in Christchurch hosting a Showtym Camp. We returned home for a camp at our own property, for which 50 riders were joining us with their ponies, and were looking forward to another four days of fun and learning. For the first two days of camp, the kids fussed over the Brumbies, excited to see them in person after following their progress on social media. They were firm favourites. While lessons were being taught, the Brumbies would stand in the middle with the kids, watching. Wondering whether Shyla would lie down in front of an audience, I gave her the signal by bending down and tapping her front leg. Within seconds, she was on the ground and rolling in the sand. One of the 12-year-olds, Olivia, asked whether she could try; curious to see how Shyla would respond to a stranger, I handed over the lead rope. Again she was down on the ground within seconds. Even Argo, Vicki's star Kaimanawa, often took longer. I was stoked — there was a real possibility that Shyla might win the Lay Down Challenge in the Battle of the Breeds in just 10 days' time, which would be pretty remarkable because everyone had picked Argo as the favourite for every category.

Some of the riders at this camp were attending for the first time, but others were regulars; kids we'd seen grow up over the years. We always loved catching up with our regular attendees. As we were too busy to ride ourselves, with so many kids to teach and entertain, and since Gaia, Shanti, Nina and Lily weren't at this camp, we asked two young riders, Katie and Kaia, whether they would like to have a few extra lessons on the Brumbies. Both were very honoured and took their responsibilities seriously. Kaia was paired with Shyla, and Katie rode Ballarat who was still very green and had only been ridden about 15 times by then.

Katie's first ride was an individual lesson riding bareback, with Amanda along to help her get used to Ballarat. Katie rode very well and displayed remarkable balance — it's very difficult to stay balanced on such a small pony without a saddle. To finish, Amanda had Katie trot into a small crossbar a few times until she was confident jumping over it.

The next day, both girls rode the Brumbies out on the arena with the other ponies. Zali, whose holiday was now over, also joined in, being led through the obstacles by one of the riders; although she hadn't recovered enough to be ridden, she was much more comfortable wearing a halter. Rather than just jump every day, exhausting and boring the horses, one day of camp always focuses on having fun, such as the riders and their ponies navigating our obstacle course, followed by a small timed challenge as a team. Ballarat and Shyla were two of the best ponies on the obstacles, having done most of them before; they bravely walked over the bridge, onto the tyres, weaved through the cones while carrying a flag, stepped onto a sinking mattress and then balanced on a box.

Next was a Tip 'n' Out jumping competition, with two categories: bareback and saddled. A few of the braver riders stripped the gear off their ponies to increase the odds of their winning, and soon the competition was under way. The jump started at 20 cm, to give Ballarat a chance to compete, and was quickly raised as the ponies jumped clear. When it got to 50 cm I watched Katie get a bit too competitive, kicking Ballarat into a canter. The poor pony, who had only cantered a few times under saddle and never into a jump, got a huge fright, leaping into the air and sending Katie flying. Jumping to her feet, she caught Ballarat and remounted, this time approaching the jump at a trot. Much happier, Ballarat cleared it easily and Katie gave her a pat before finishing. Shyla was still jumping clear, but not wanting to overwhelm her with a strange rider on I called Kaia over after they had cleared 80 cm and suggested that she end on a good note. Nodding, Kaia gave Shyla a pat and walked her around the arena, letting Shyla stretch her head long and low as they cooled off.

Camp was good for all three ponies, although somewhat tiring; we gave them two days in the paddock to recover. They now had just four days before we made the long journey south to Equidays, at Mystery Creek near Hamilton, and all of them were exactly at the stage they needed to be: we were sure that they wouldn't be overwhelmed by the crowds or the atmosphere, and nor would they object to being patted by strangers during the Meet and Greets — camp had been good practice for them. Just before we left, Nina and her sister Lily, came out for a final lesson. It was Nina's last chance to ride Shyla before the decision about buying her back needed to be made. I was 100 per cent sure what I wanted; now it was up to Nina to decide whether she'd be Shyla's rider. Having seen them together many times over the past few months, it was obvious that Nina loved Shyla as much as I did and that Shyla worked well for her, but I wanted them to have one more ride together just to be sure it was the right fit; Nina would be riding Shyla more than I would in the coming years, so it was important that she could see Shyla fitting into her future.

We finished the lesson with a quick Tip 'n' Out competition; it was an easy way for Nina to get used to cantering Shyla into the jumps and also give her the opportunity to try her over a few bigger fences without tiring the mare. The oxer started at about 65 cm and both girls jumped it with ease. With each round I increased the height by 10 cm, and soon it was 95 cm. Lily approached it first; although the rail stayed up, her pony nudged it just a little with her hooves. If Nina could clear the jump, she'd be the winner. Shyla cantered in with her ears pricked forward, her rhythm remaining consistent. At take-off the little Brumby tucked her knees up and flew over the jump with room to spare. With a huge grin, Nina settled back in the saddle and brought Shyla back to a long-rein walk.

After giving Shyla a huge hug, Nina dismounted. We led the ponies back to the stables to unsaddle them; then, turning to me, she couldn't contain her delight as she said that she would love to help me with the next chapter of Shyla's training and that maybe, just like me, one day she could write a book about her adventures with Shyla. Until this moment I hadn't realised that Nina and I shared a love of writing, and I started asking questions. Amazingly, this 10-year-old was already a published author, on Amazon, and had earned $100 from her first three books. Blown away, I left the girls to unsaddle and put the ponies away while I hurried back to the house and downloaded her books; I had some reading to do!

CHAPTER 21
Battle of the Breeds

Equidays weekend arrived, and seemingly before we knew it we had 12 horses unloaded from their trucks and safely tucked into their yards at Mystery Creek. As ambassadors for the event it was a huge show for us, and we were especially excited to have all three wild horse breeds to showcase together! Apart from Shyla, Argo and Bragg competing in the Battle of the Breeds show, Amanda had Bragg competing in the 1.10-metre Derby, we had two horses in the Grand Prix on Friday night, three horses in the Grand Prix Derby, and Instigator and Mascot in the Kaimanawa Stallion Challenges — and Gaia and Shanti were also showcasing the two Kaimanawa fillies they'd trained.

Spotlight had also joined us for his famous performance as Pegasus, one last time before he retired. He was heading south to spend his last years trekking in the hills near Hastings and being pampered by his new owners. With Argo having learnt everything, and more, that Spotlight did, the older gelding was going to enjoy a quiet life while his younger protégé took over many of the public demonstrations and also assisted Vicki in training any wild or difficult horses that arrived at the property.

Before Equidays began, we had an afternoon in a park in nearby Cambridge so that members of the public could meet Argo and Spotlight. This would be followed by the premiere screening of *Mustang Ride*, a movie about our adventures taming wild horses in America the winter before. Like always, Vicki's horses won the hearts of the people gathered at the park, as did Dan Steers and his Australian Stock Horse Double Image, an equine celebrity in his own right, who had just flown into the country from Australia for Equidays. Leaving Mum to load the horses and return them to the showgrounds, the rest of us piled into the car, getting changed, doing our hair and touching up our make-up while we drove to the cinema. We arrived just in time, and had an awesome evening: sharing our favourite memories from America, signing books, and then watching *Mustang Ride*; previously, we'd only seen rough edits and never in chronological order. We were incredibly proud of Amanda, who had filmed and directed the documentary, and also incredibly thankful that she'd captured it all on camera. Seeing it brought back a lot of good memories and we felt so nostalgic; we were missing the horses, the people and America more than ever. There is no doubt that it was one of the best times of our lives.

We woke early the next morning to prepare Mascot and Instigator for their Handling and Conditioning class of the Kaimanawa Stallion Challenges; Vicki finished second and Alexa fifth. The afternoon was spent doing book signings and then clinics, with all three of us teaching in our respective fields: Vicki's was working with young and sore horses, Amanda focused on rider position and sports psychology, and I worked with photography enthusiasts and did book readings. It was a busy first day for us, and the evening was even busier.

Amanda had been asked to compete Bragg in the Speed Slalom, a competition that pitches one horse against another in the ultimate display of speed over a small course of jumps. As Bragg had only competed at one show before, Amanda was worried that he would be stressed by being in the indoor arena in front of 2500 spectators. The organisers were sympathetic, and paired her up in the first round with our good friend Warwick Schiller, who was visiting from America. A renowned horse trainer, Warwick normally used a Western saddle but had gamely agreed to attempt showjumping on a borrowed horse. Not wanting to overwhelm Bragg, Amanda took him around the course quietly and the brave little pony valiantly jumped around clear. In the ring beside her, Warwick had survived a near fall at the start flags but recovered well, speedily navigating the rest of the course to finish clear and in a faster time than Amanda.

With Bragg out of the Speed Slalom, Amanda turned her attention to her showjumper. She was competing in the Grand Prix on Showtym Cassanova, while Vicki would be riding Ngahiwi Showtym Premier. For both, it was their first show of the season and a lot was riding on how well they competed; we'd recently announced that we were forming Team WS — a joint-ownership venture to acquire a team of horses capable of competing on the world stage — and knew that many people would be watching to see whether the girls were at the top of their game.

Both pairs jumped clear. Vicki's round was documented in a world-first — she'd been wearing a 360-degree camera helmet and it made for quite a trippy playback. In the second round, a dropped rail knocked Vicki out of the placings but Amanda jumped a fast clear round, catapulting her and Cassanova to the top of the leader board, and they returned to the arena for the prize-giving as the winners. Vicki redeemed herself the following day by jumping a double clear on Premier to place second in the Grand Prix Derby, with Amanda finishing fourth. It was a great weekend for the showjumpers.

Also on the Saturday, Bragg the Mustang exceeded all expectations in his Derby; although he was the smallest horse in the field, he simply flew around the challenging course. Considering that he'd only jumped a handful of times in America, of which only once had been over coloured poles, it was remarkable how far this Mustang had progressed since arriving in New Zealand four months earlier. Amanda couldn't have been more pleased.

That afternoon, our Brumbies stood in front of thousands of people as we talked about our work in Australia and the plight the horses were facing. While we talked, we led the horses along the fence line letting people pat them. Although initially hesitant, the horses soon gained confidence and enjoyed greeting their fans.

Now the only event left for the day was Bragg, Shyla and Argo competing in the Battle of the Breeds that night. We made sure that all three had lots of rest before they had to head back to the arena. Again, 2500 people filled the grandstands; Alexa welcomed them and got the crowd clapping and stamping their feet in time to Queen's song 'We Will Rock You'. The stadium shook as we entered the arena in formation, carrying the flags of each of the nations where the horses had once roamed wild. Argo and Vicki boldly led the way, unfazed by either the noise or the lights, Bragg and Amanda pranced behind them, and Shyla hesitantly followed with me, having never seen anything like it in her life.

Coming to a halt in the centre of the ring, we raised our flags in a salute to the crowds; I kept a firm hold on the reins to keep Shyla still when the arena erupted into thunderous applause. Beside us, Bragg pawed at the air; further over Argo was standing still, proudly carrying the New Zealand flag. Then the challenges got under way. The first was for the riders: each of us had 60 seconds to introduce our horse and explain more about the plight of the wild horses in their particular countries. Amanda took the win, by talking about the Mustangs with a near-perfect American accent — by popular demand, she managed to maintain the accent throughout the evening.

The next round was Best Sidepass, which to my surprise Shyla won. Although Argo actually performed better, the judges — Warwick Schiller and Dan Steers — said they had to allow for him having had more than two years of training, and that they were impressed with how well Shyla had progressed in such a short time. Next came Best Canter to Halt, to the sound of 'Stop Right Now' by the Spice Girls; again Shyla won, stopping perfectly in sync with the lyrics. The horses then competed in Best Jump. Shyla made a gallant effort, clearing 1 metre before I retired her gracefully. Vicki and Amanda had been handicapped by the judges for this round, and were required to compete bareback; Bragg was the eventual winner.

Just three more rounds remained, with Shyla and Bragg on two points and Argo on one point. Hoping to gain favour with the judges, Vicki leant forward and removed her bridle for Best Turn on the Haunches (or Spin), and sitting perfectly balanced she and Argo performed an extravagant Western spin with no gear to aid them. Admitting defeat, Amanda and I forfeited the round and we progressed to the next, Best Rear. This was supposed to be Bragg's moment to shine, but when Amanda dismounted to cue him he trotted away. This made Argo the winner, as Shyla had never been taught to rear on cue; it seemed like a terrible thing to train a kid's pony to do!

With the horses now on equal points, there was just one challenge left. Whoever won Best Lay Down would be the overall winner. In practice Shyla had refused to lie down, unsettled by the new arena, but for the past few minutes she'd been dropping her head and buckling at the knees; I'd had to keep her moving to stop her lying down with me sitting on her! I quickly dismounted and removed the saddle — as soon as we were given the go-ahead from the judges, Shyla was on the ground and rolling, enjoying the soft sand beneath her. Argo, who was still bareback and bridleless, lay down smartly to voice command; and Amanda, who had not trained Bragg for this, lay down herself in the sand, much to the amusement of the crowd.

The judges deemed Shyla to be the winner, but when Argo lay down flat and then rose into a sitting position, it went to a public vote. Argo was declared the winner and the overall champion of Battle of the Breeds. It was a well-contested victory for the New Zealand horse; he'd won on home soil and the audience couldn't have been happier.

It had been two years since Vicki had competed Argo at Equidays in the very first Stallion Challenges, finishing as Reserve Champion in the Ridden Freestyle and also in the overall rankings. Looking back, we realised how special their pairing was. No other Kaimanawa in the country was as big — at 16 hands high, Argo was not only an amazing example of what Kaimanawas are capable of, but also a practical height for Vicki to keep in the long term. Most of the wild horses we work with are only ponies, which makes it hard to have a long-term future with them. For Argo to be both big and talented was even more remarkable. Watching Vicki jump Argo 1.30 metres bareback and bridleless has always been amazing. As young as he was, there was no telling what he'd be capable of in the coming years.

Every wild horse we work with is given the same opportunity to be as special as Argo; the love and time we invest in them is the same regardless of what they can give us. Often, though, their height, age, conformation, nature or soundness can limit their potential, and we have to adjust our training to focus on each horse as an individual. Vicki's current Kaimanawa, Mascot, had a limited future because of the injuries he'd sustained in the wild, and his level of training in the Stallion Challenges at Equidays reflected this. Although he couldn't jump, and would go unsound if cantered for more than a few strides or ridden on the hills, he had a sweet nature that allowed kids to handle him and was safe to ride bareback, lie all over, carry things and drag things off. He also loved to lie down; quietly watching everything while he rested his weary body. Although Mascot was restricted in his capabilities, Vicki had found a future for him where he could thrive; at Equidays she focused on showcasing his lovely nature, giving the public a chance to meet him before he went to live with a family of young kids that Vicki had gifted him to as a lead-rein pony.

Alexa's horse, Instigator, also had limitations as to what he was capable of, and so she also focused on what he excelled at. Like Mascot, Instigator was quiet and easy to work with — Alexa was able to stand on his back, carry things and walk and trot him around on a loose rein. Not once did she ask him something that he wasn't 100 per cent comfortable doing, and in the ring this was obvious; they were the only combination that showcased faultlessly, and although they didn't canter he looked incredibly relaxed and happy. To our surprise, Alexa wasn't marked down for not showing all three paces and they were announced as the class winners. Vicki and Mascot, who'd placed consistently in all four classes, finished third overall, with Alexa and Instigator fifth. To our delight Vicki was awarded Fan Favourite for the second year; it was a fitting tribute to Mascot, who had fully embraced his life with humans.

Exhausted after three huge days, we sat down with friends to reflect over a great show. The horses had done well, the book signings had been hugely popular (it had taken more than six hours to get through everyone), and we'd made some great friends; including Dan, who we were looking forward to catching up with in just three weeks' time at Equitana when we went over for the Australian Brumby Challenge.

CHAPTER 22

Olympic Dreams

When we got back home, the property was in the middle of a make-over. Six months earlier, the home property, where Amanda's and my horses were based, had been re-fenced with Equine Fence Wire supplied by one of our sponsors, Gallagher, to make it safer for the horses; now the paddocks surrounding Vicki's stables were also being done. We were just days away from having three valuable new showjumpers arriving from overseas and needed to ensure that they had safe paddocks to enjoy. Vicki's property also wasn't set up for stallions, and with two coming, the re-fencing also gave her the opportunity to redesign the layout of her paddocks and put in higher fences where needed.

The three new horses were the first of 10 that would be jointly owned by Team WS; an innovative initiative that would enable Vicki and Amanda to work towards achieving their dreams of showjumping at international level. For the past decade, ever since they'd competed in their first Grand Prix classes, both girls had strived to produce élite showjumpers and they had enjoyed huge successes over the years. Horses like Showtym Girl, Witheze, Wurlitzer, Showtym Viking, Showtym Levado GNZ, Showtym Cadet MVNZ, Ngahiwi Showtym Premier, Showtym Cassanova and Caretino Jewel had established them as some of the nation's most competitive and successful riders, with wins right through to both Super League and World Cup level. However, while these horses were competitive in

New Zealand, most weren't of the calibre needed to compete against the best in the world.

Unlike many riders, whose access to big budgets allows them to purchase horses that are already competing at the biggest heights, Vicki and Amanda had spent years producing horses that other people had given up on, or wildcards with no notable breeding that had proven to be fantastic jumpers. All of their World Cup jumpers had cost between $500 and $7000; they had never been in a sufficiently strong financial position to afford more. While we had no doubt that their team of horses, which was improving year by year, would eventually produce showjumpers capable of campaigning on the world stage, the Team WS initiative was making this possible years earlier.

In late August, Vicki and Amanda had travelled to the other side of the world to select the first horses. Vicki chose two four-year-old stallions, one an approved Holstein by the name of Daminos, from the United Kingdom, and the other a grey Zangersheide called Carpaccio BDV Z, from Belgium. The third horse, chosen by Amanda, was Quintesse Z, a stunning chestnut Zangersheide mare from Holland; she was an absolute powerhouse with an incredible jump. Never in a million years had Amanda imagined that she would ride a horse of that quality, and she was so thankful to the first 40 owners for joining Team WS and making it possible. Eventually, with the full team of 250 owners behind us, Vicki and Amanda would be training a team of horses specifically with the Olympics in mind. The plan was that within two years all 10 horses would be on the team, competing at the top of their game, in what we hope will be one of the most exciting teams of showjumpers this nation has ever seen.

Two days after our return from Equidays, the Gallagher fencing was complete and we could barely recognise our property. Although our previous fencing was reasonably horse-friendly, we could see what an improvement the new fencing made, highlighting several areas where it had previously been less than ideal. Even avoiding a single accident would justify changing the fencing over. Our property looked like a show home.

With the fencing completed on time, we all piled into the truck for the drive to Auckland to collect the new horses from the airport. Alexa and I would be seeing them for the first time. The groom who'd travelled with them was the same one who had flown over with us and the Brumbies; we had a moment of déjà vu — less than four months earlier we'd also been unloading three horses off a plane, but horses of a completely different breed and for a completely different purpose.

The groom grinned at us and joked about the quality of these horses compared with the Brumbies, and as we watched Vicki and Amanda unload them we couldn't help but laugh at the difference, too. These sleek, high-strung beauties were nothing like the dull, hairy Brumbies we'd led down the ramp a few months ago. As each horse was led past us and loaded onto the waiting truck, however, our laughter changed to awe. We've had some exceptional horses over the years, but never had we seen three horses with such presence. Although we'd seen countless photos and videos of them, it was nothing like seeing them in the flesh; Vicki and Amanda had selected well, and we knew that their owners would be just as excited when they saw them.

On arriving home, Vicki settled the stallions into stables, while Quintesse, Amanda's mare, was led straight out to a paddock. She was very lean from her six weeks in quarantine and from the travelling; for her, the only job for the next month was to rest and regain the weight she'd lost. The stallions were soon out in paddocks as well; Carpaccio who'd grown up in a field, was in his element and quickly settled down to graze. For Daminos, though, this was a novel experience, as for the past nine months the only time he'd left his box was to be exercised in an indoor arena. For the first week, he would nervously wait at the gate, keen to be back in the confinement of his stable, although he soon adjusted to New Zealand life. Both stallions had remarkable temperaments and were settling in well. Every day when we looked out to the paddock and saw these horses, we'd shake our heads in disbelief, amazed that the Team WS concept was now a reality.

It seems fitting that our work with the wild horses first began because of our showjumpers, when, back in 2012, the Kaimanawa Watch Me

Move won Pony of the Year — the most prestigious Pony Grand Prix event in the Southern Hemisphere. Ever since then, our journey with wild horses across three different continents has attracted widespread public interest that has led to international recognition of our efforts, although it still surprises us when people know us for our work with wild horses rather than showjumpers. The showjumpers remain Vicki and Amanda's core focus and passion, consuming nine months of every year. Now, because of the public following we have attracted through the wild horses, it has come full circle with support for our Olympic dreams.

It was especially exciting to start with young horses, four-year-olds, so that they could be trained our way right from the beginning. The process of training our performance horses doesn't differ from that of our wild ones; they all get started bareback in a halter, all learn to be ridden out over the farm, and all enjoy beach rides and swimming in the river — a far cry from how most showjumpers begin their careers. The differences between wild horses and élite sport horses might be diverse, but one thing is true for them all: whether we're starting a wild Brumby or a Warmblood for the jumping arena, for us it's all about building a solid and trusting foundation based on love and kindness.

Vicki's two stallions quickly learnt to become real horses; not shut away in boxes, but instead enjoying the freedom of large paddocks during the day. At night, they were brought in to Vicki's specially designed stables with an open aisle and open walls so that the horses could be included in the daily comings and goings. Although it took a week for the stallions to adjust to the many changes, they settled in and were often found scratching the backs of the geldings stabled alongside them. Daminos, whose stable was nearest the entry to the barn, would often pop his head over his door to greet people as they came in, or watch as horses were saddled in the aisle. He was learning to be socialised; something that was vital to the sanity of a competition stallion and was in stark contrast to the solitary confinement they were often used to overseas.

A few weeks after the Team WS horses arrived, Daminos — who'd had 15 rides in the UK — headed out for his first ride with us. It was his very first time out of an indoor arena, or with company, but he boldly led the other horses out on the farm, eager to explore the world. Carpaccio's first ride was also spent cantering around the farm under saddle, and although he didn't put a foot wrong he was decidedly wobblier. Vicki called his breeder to see how much ridden work he'd done. She'd been told that he had been started under saddle, and so assumed that he'd been ridden, but quickly discovered that he'd only been sat on a few times and always on a lead rein. Taking Carpaccio back to the basics, she started him again; first lying over him bareback to get him used to the feel of a rider, then spending a few days riding bareback, getting him comfortably walking, trotting and cantering on the arena, before resaddling him. In between rides, Carpaccio learnt to swim in the river, joining our other showjumpers for fitness laps. Quintesse, who had never been ridden, continued to laze in the paddock — she would have a full month to rest before Amanda started the backing process.

In between working the Team WS horses, the Brumbies went through their final preparations for Equitana. Zali, who'd been withdrawn from the competition due to her soundness issues, was now running with a Welsh stallion; we hoped that 18 months in a paddock would give her teeth time to settle. If, after that time, she was sound and happy, Vicki would then continue to train her for ridden work; if not, she would have a good home regardless — she was a beautiful and sweet mare who deserved to live happily ever after.

Ballarat, who'd only had about 20 rides, was now making rapid progress. The extra time spent to get her healthy and happy meant that her handling was well established; it often felt as if Amanda was working with a young domestic pony rather than a wild one. Ballarat kept showing a willingness to learn that impressed us, and Amanda was really enjoying working with her again, although the pony was still very inexperienced and unpredictable at times, and Amanda fell off her twice. Two weeks before the Brumbies were due to fly back to Australia, we took Ballarat and Shyla to a Show Hunter training day. Shyla behaved like a pro, jumping around a 90-cm course, and Ballarat also exceeded every expectation. Amanda first warmed her up over a single fence, gradually increasing it from a pole on the ground up to 50 cm, then Ballarat happily trotted into the arena and jumped around a small course.

With our flights to Australia now only two weeks away, we realised that we had no plans for the four days leading up to the competition. We originally thought we'd be based at Colleen's, which was three hours away, but this seemed like unnecessary extra travelling time for our ponies. I contacted our new friend, Dan, to see whether he knew anyone we could stay with. He quickly organised for a family to collect the Brumbies from the airport and for us to stay at their equestrian property 40 minutes from the showgrounds. Moza, their young daughter, was an aspiring showjumper and a huge fan of our TV show *Keeping Up With The Kaimanawas*. When she heard that we were coming to visit she started looking through all our Brumby photos on Facebook and immediately fell in love with Ballarat. When we got an e-mail from Moza's mum asking about buying Ballarat, we crossed our fingers that she would suit their family. We'd been praying that she would be auctioned off to a perfect home, and now it looked as if we might have found one. Moza had been riding her entire life; she was gutsy, used to working with young and difficult ponies and, more importantly, loved Brumbies. Although she'd recently moved on to a 14-hand pony and had dreams of competing at Grand Prix level, she was searching for a fun pony to trail-ride on — every year, the family camped for a week in Barmah National Park to visit the Brumbies.

After talking at great length, and seeing videos and photos, Amanda was confident that Moza would provide the right home for Ballarat; now she just needed to ensure that Ballarat was the right pony for Moza. Shanti, who hadn't ridden Ballarat for a couple of months, jumped at the chance to come out and ride her again. She, Gaia, Nina and Lily all came to stay for a week. Nina rode Shyla and Shanti rode Ballarat; first doing lessons, then riding out on the farm and swimming in the river. In between rides, the kids helped me work on Shyla's costume, which had a snow theme to honour her Snowy Mountain heritage.

In the last week leading up to the challenge, Amanda hopped on Ballarat bareback, with just a rope around her neck. The little mare soon understood the neck cues, walking and trotting around the arena like a schoolmistress horse. While Amanda had no intention of including this skill — something she'd only tried at the last minute — in her freestyle component for the competition, it was incredibly rewarding for her to see Ballarat's potential for working bridleless. It was a true reflection of the trust Amanda had developed with her. The little bay Brumby had only had about 30 rides, as opposed to Shyla who'd had about 100, but Amanda was confident that with a little more time she'd be a very fun and competitive pony.

CHAPTER 23

The Passing of a Legend

In that last week before we were due to fly to Australia, tragedy struck. Vicki's favourite Kaimanawa, Argo, showed very mild signs of distress after he'd been for a farm ride; when he didn't respond to treatment, Vicki called the vet.

Within an hour of the vet treating him, Argo's appetite returned, and for the first time in hours Vicki felt comfortable leaving his side. At 9 p.m. that night she joined us for a late dinner, and half an hour later she checked him again — he was happily munching on hay and gave her a nudge when she checked him over. Vicki, who slept in a loft above the stables, headed to bed thinking that the worst was over — but less than an hour later, she awoke to hear Argo moving about, unsettled, in his stable below.

Rushing downstairs, she ran to her horse and tried to calm him, but there was little she could do. She rang for help, waking everyone up, but even with three people it was difficult to hold him still. He was quickly losing control of his body and was struggling to stand, often falling to the ground. Vicki managed to give him pain relief, and he finally lay still as we all waited for the vets to reach our property; it was almost midnight and the drive would take at least 45 minutes. By the time the vets arrived, there was nothing they could do to save him and he was put to sleep; he died just as he had lived, surrounded by the people he loved, and in Vicki's arms.

Argo's loss shook all of us deeply; we've had some incredible horses over the years, but none quite like him. From the moment he arrived from the wild, Argo had a love for humans that was a privilege to be part of, none more so than for Vicki, who became the centre of his world. His ability to enjoy life shone through every day, and he always made the people around him smile; he brought fun, freedom, love and laughter wherever he went. Argo's intelligence and gentleness won the hearts of people across the nation, and the number of lives he touched over the years was reflective of just how much room he had to love; his patience with his fans knew no bounds.

For the next few days we walked around in a blur, unable to comprehend why our gentle giant had been taken so young. The loss was especially hard for Vicki as he'd been far more than just a horse to her — in many ways he was her best friend and her confidant. She trusted him explicitly, not only when sitting astride his back but also with her secrets and dreams. Losing Argo was like losing a child, and it left a gaping hole in our family; even the slightest mention of him would bring tears. All over the country, people seemed to understand our pain. Meals were delivered by friends, flowers were sent and drawings of Argo were posted to us in the mail. For days, we lost all inspiration for riding and for life in general, and spent most of our days grieving; working the Brumbies was the last thing on our minds just then.

AMANDA AND I SOON HAD TO RETURN our attention to the Brumbies; for Vicki, it was the Team WS horses that got her back on a horse and excited about something. The distraction was sorely needed, and having something to focus on gave Vicki a purpose again. On her first ride on Daminos after Argo's death, the striking stallion worked beautifully; and then, as she was cooling him off, he dropped his head down into the sand and collapsed softly beneath her, lying down much like Argo used to do. It was behaviour so unlike that of an élite performance horse and in so many ways a reminder of Argo that it left us shaken. In the days that followed, Daminos really came into his own. Argo's spirit seemed to shine through the young

Holstein stallion, especially in the river, where Vicki was able to stand on his back as he trotted lengths. Hearing Vicki laugh again was a relief for everyone.

All too soon we were due at the airport with Shyla and Ballarat. As the flight clashed with a World Cup show, I headed over to Australia alone with the Brumbies, staying with friends in Auckland the night before the flight; Vicki and Amanda would follow a few days later after they had competed. The 2 a.m. start from our friends' place left much to be desired, and there was a lot of waiting around at the airport for the Brumbies to be loaded onto the plane, together with a young racehorse. Finally, we were in the air at 6 a.m. and I collapsed in my seat behind the cockpit of the cargo plane, exhausted. Three hours later I woke with a start; the plane was descending, and I listened as the pilots counted down the landing. The groom had checked on the horses while I'd been asleep, and all was well. Once we were on the tarmac I was a little apprehensive; we were being collected by total strangers and I could only hope they had remembered to pick us up.

I stood at the front of the horses' stalls as the cargo box was driven to the unloading corral. Rain and torrential wind shook the box, and the canvas roof was flapping wildly. The Brumbies remained relaxed, but the young racehorse was spooked. They unloaded the racehorse first, onto the wet tarmac; the Brumbies were held while the stressed thoroughbred was led to a waiting transporter. Full of tension, it danced sideways, half rearing on its lead, nervous about loading onto a strange truck. It took 20 minutes and a sedation before the young horse gained enough courage to walk up the ramp, but finally it was the Brumbies' turn to load onto a strange vehicle. Just like at home, they were on within seconds and soon we were on the highway, navigating the rush-hour traffic as we headed away from Melbourne. While we drove I chatted with Danielle, our host, about her family and their horses, and the more I heard the more excited I became. There was a real possibility that Moza would suit Ballarat, and I knew how much relief Amanda would feel if she knew in advance who might be bidding. After 40 minutes of driving we arrived at Danielle's property, and my jaw dropped; it was a horse paradise, with 100 acres of beautifully fenced paddocks, stables, arenas and horses as far as the eye could see. What really impressed me, though, was hearing how often they rode in the You Yangs Regional Park, which bordered the property and was set up with bridle paths on which to ride the horses.

We settled the Brumbies into a paddock so that they could stretch their legs after their flight, and I headed for bed to catch up on sleep. When I woke some time later, I went outside to check the horses and meet Moza. She soon won me over with her stories of riding — she had a zest for life and huge dreams, reminding me of Vicki when she was younger; I had a good feeling about her. The next day we caught the ponies and saddled up for a ride; although Amanda wasn't there, it gave Moza a chance to get to ride Ballarat and see how they got on.

We started in the small round pen, as I was cautious about having a 10-year-old I didn't know on such a green, once-wild pony. Ballarat was still reactive at times, and I didn't want to risk giving her, or Moza, a fright. They began walking and were soon trotting; when the arena door banged shut, Ballarat leapt forward and spun around in fright, but rather than panicking, her little rider laughed and patted her, telling Ballarat she was silly for being scared. Many kids would have panicked and hopped off at that point, or snatched at the reins and frightened the pony further, so I was very impressed with Moza's incredible feel and relaxed manner. Confident that she was ready for more, I opened the gate and we headed out to a paddock, trotting through fields of long grass. Ballarat was brave and led the way, while Shyla had to be convinced that an old tree trunk wouldn't kill her, and nor would the black water troughs that lined the races.

After Moza had had her first canter, she circled, grinning, over to where I waited on Shyla and asked whether we could head out into the You Yangs. Initially I'd been unsure about heading out into the open with a young pony and a young kid, but after watching her ride Ballarat for the past 20 minutes I was sure it would be fine. A friend of Moza's joined us, and together we rode through the towering gum trees in search of logs to jump.

Ballarat took the lead, and I told Moza to choose a pace she was comfortable with. A brisk trot soon turned into a slow canter, and as we wove between the gums Ballarat kept her ears perked, loving the adventure. Beneath me Shyla was also relaxed, enjoying the ride. I wondered whether the smell of gum trees and the kangaroos — both of which they obviously hadn't come across for some months — made them feel at home. Shortly afterwards we came to a crossroads in the track and Moza fell back to a walk. At the edge of the trees was an obstacle made of tyres, which I thought would be good practice for the Brumbies before the competition. Ballarat and Shyla, who were both quite bold now, bravely stepped their hooves into each tyre. A small log attracted our attention and we turned and trotted over it, but as it was too small for the ponies to jump we headed deeper into the trees, following a sandy riverbed until we came across a fallen tree.

Moza went first; Ballarat jumped the tree smartly before turning and jumping it again and again. Both Moza and her friend were having heaps of fun, and I tried to hold Shyla steady while I photographed them from the ground. Behind me Shyla was twitching and swishing her tail, but it wasn't until I felt insects biting me that I realised she was covered in giant mosquitoes. Quickly mounting again I followed the girls over the log before we hightailed it back and washed the ponies off before putting them away.

It was a huge relief having seen Moza handle and ride Ballarat. If she decided that Ballarat would fit into their family, the pony would land on her feet. It was sheer luck that Dan had organised us to stay with a family that had not only a small rider but also one who wanted a new pony; even better, she rode at a higher level than most kids of her age. I had a feeling it was meant to be, and I couldn't wait for Amanda to see them together when she and Vicki flew in the following day.

I was at the airport early to meet them, and the three of us then spent the morning at the ABC studios, being interviewed by radio stations across Australia. My first two books had been reprinted as an omnibus edition and been released in Australia a week earlier, and this gave us a fabulous opportunity to both promote it and talk about our current work with the Brumbies. We arrived at Moza's late in the afternoon and saddled up for a ride in the indoor arena. It would be our last schooling session before the competition began, and our last chance to work through everything the ponies would be doing in each of their four classes.

Shyla was hesitant and spooky, and I had one of my worst rides on her; but Ballarat was a little superstar, working well on the flat for the first 10 minutes. Amanda, who was more interested in ensuring that Ballarat had a good future than in competing well over the next four days, asked Moza if she wanted another ride on Ballarat; she did. Instead of schooling her, Amanda put the pair of them through their paces, before jumping over some small jumps. Like me, Amanda was blown away by Moza's talent and attitude.

CHAPTER 24

Australian Brumby Challenge

Arriving at Equitana for the Australian Brumby Challenge was a strange feeling; in many ways, it was an anti-climax. With Moza and Ballarat paired up and hopefully successful in the auction, and Shyla coming home with me to be competed by Nina, I felt as if we were already winners. Regardless of how the next few days went, the outcomes for both ponies were already the best possible scenarios. Competing was now just an opportunity to show the 40,000 people coming through the gates how special Brumbies are.

Once the horses were settled in their stables, we set off to find the Double Dans — the Dan we'd met at Equidays was one of a duo of internationally renowned Australian horse trainers. The other, Dan James, had flown over from America, where he is now based, with his family for Equitana. Not only would they be doing clinics over the whole four days, but they were also sharing the arena with us for the opening night's show, Flight Without Wings, in front of thousands of people. We would all be using the Double Dan horses for this show — a huge ask since we'd never even met them before. Luckily the horses were well trained and knew exactly what they were doing, and Dan Steers had prepared a fun and interactive plan for the evening event; after a few practices, we were confident that we'd be able to entertain the audience.

The next afternoon the Brumbies had their first class: Handling and Conditioning. Both Amanda and I were happy with our horses — they stood to be caught, picked up their feet nicely and then loaded onto the horse trailer like pros. Ballarat's loading was beautifully executed, and I thought that there was a good chance they'd place well, so was surprised when neither of us finished in the top six. It wasn't until we saw the scoresheets that we realised we'd been marked down for leaving the rope on the ground while we picked up the horses' feet; while we had thought that this showed how quietly the horses were standing, they had judged it as a sign of poor horsemanship and we'd lost significant amounts of marks.

After the class we turned our focus to the evening performance, running through a final practice. Hoping that we were ready, we waited backstage while the Double Dans did an opening act, then we entered the arena for a challenge of sorts: they shared their passion for reining and freestyles with us, then dared us to give it a go; then in turn we shared our passion for showjumping with them and taught Dan Steers and Double Image to jump — with Dan eventually clearing 1.05 metres, which was pretty impressive for someone who had never worn jodhpurs or ridden in an English saddle before. As the heights increased, the three of us continued jumping, with Vicki and Amanda jumping bareback to 1.40 metres. Next, the Dans brought two horses out to sit on a bean bag and Vicki borrowed the horse I'd been riding and jumped over them. To close the show, Moza and two of her friends joined us to create a dream sequence. The three little girls came out with a miniature chestnut horse and acted us playing with our ponies as children and dreaming of taming horses; it ended with the pony sitting down and all three of them sleeping around him. The lights went out; when they came up, it was to see us, as adults, sleeping beside one of Dan's chestnut Quarter Horses — we 'woke', and together repeated what the girls had done but on a larger scale to show how our childhood dreams with horses had come true. It was a fantastic night, and we thoroughly enjoyed working with the Double Dans to make it happen.

When I warmed Shyla up for her second class the following morning,

I was relieved that she already had a home — never before had she been so diabolical! No one watching would ever have thought that she was suitable for kids; I shook my head in exasperation at the irony of it. At their challenge events, neither my Kaimanawa nor my Mustang had shown to the level they were trained to, and now it seemed that my Brumby was going to do the same. I watched other Brumbies at the far end of the warm-up ring working perfectly, relaxed and confident as they worked through their paces; among them was Ballarat, who'd never looked better. I was so distracted with trying to relax Shyla that I completely forgot the workout routine I was about to perform, and as I struggled to remember it I ended up in tears. Amanda had been watching me, and now rode over and offered to ride in front of me so that I could follow her through the pattern. It was amazing how stressful a simple routine had become, and I tried to shake off my nerves; Shyla already had a home, so it really didn't matter how she performed.

Just minutes before I was due in the arena, the class was delayed for 30 minutes. I continued to work Shyla in, and the extra time made all the difference; within 10 minutes, my stressed and reactive pony was working softly and quietly — she was back to the Shyla I recognised! We made our way to the arena and I let Shyla rest before the Pattern class began. We were the first to go, and from the moment we entered the arena Shyla felt good, working accurately through her transitions. As I rode out at the end of our turn I was so happy; it couldn't possibly have gone better, especially after the awful warm-up. Amanda was next, and it was the opposite for her: Ballarat might have warmed up perfectly, but she was agitated in the arena. Very quickly it became obvious that her tongue was over the bit, causing her discomfort. I ran over to the gate steward to ask if Amanda could fix the bridle and start again and they agreed, calling her out of the ring. By the time the pair re-entered, Ballarat was still a little fussy about the contact but worked well. It was disappointing after how consistently she'd been working over the past few weeks, but Amanda was very pleased at how well she'd performed in front of crowds of people considering just how little experience she had.

The next class was the Obstacle. Again it didn't go quite to plan, although both ponies put in a pretty solid effort. The course involved opening a gate, backing between poles, jumping, climbing over a bridge, ground tying and dragging a log around a cone. I was first to go again, and Shyla aced everything except the dragging, which we'd never had issues with when practising at home, but I made a few rider errors. Rather than pulling the log so that the rope was kept off the horse, I let it pull against her rump, upsetting her. Amanda, and every other rider, learnt from my mistake and were careful to pull in the better direction, although some horses couldn't cope at all and many riders continued past without completing the obstacle.

In between watching us in the classes for the Brumbies, Vicki didn't have a minute spare. Each day she would educate the public on horse welfare and horsemanship, and she also competed in the Celebrity Couples challenge, pairing up with our good friend Warwick Schiller as his wife had been unable to fly over from America. Vicki's sore horse clinics were particularly well received; as in New Zealand, people were impressed by the extensive knowledge she was able to share on teeth, splints, saddle fit, nutrition, sheath cleaning, hoof balance and skeletal issues. Many of the showjumping riders, who knew of us from competing in New Zealand or when Vicki rode in Australia, were so impressed that they asked if she would look over their competition horses who were due to compete in the World Cup that night. One by one she examined horses and identified issues that explained much of the symptoms they were seeing; the horses she worked on finished in the top four placings later that night, and the owners were very happy.

Going into the fourth and final class, the Freestyle, on the last day, was something I was looking forward to. Nina, Lily, Gaia and Shanti had helped make Shyla a snowflake costume, and I'd designed a workout that incorporated everything Shyla enjoyed. Once again I was the first to go and Shyla was foot-perfect. Although still green, she performed better than I had expected and I was so proud of her. In addition to the basics, I had shown a side pass, jumped Shyla to 90 cm and carried a billowing flag and a ball, as well as executing canter-to-halt and halt-to-canter transitions and a turn on the haunches.

Amanda was next in, and she too aced her Freestyle. Ballarat did much of what Shyla had done, though her billowing flag was twice as big and she also stood while a ball was rolled between her legs. Amanda was proud of her pony, as were we all: both horses had demonstrated to the public the potential of wild Brumbies and had produced some of the most well-rounded Freestyles of any of the wild horses we had trained. Thrilled with the ponies, we returned to the ring to watch everyone else compete and were amazed by the high level of training: horse after horse continued to raise the bar, and the Freestyles got better and better.

The Brumbies' remarkable ability to stay relaxed and perform at such a high level stood out; more of them were able to produce a polished and crowd-pleasing workout than the Mustangs or Kaimanawas we'd seen in similar events. In addition, the percentage of horses originally assigned to trainers that had made it through to the competition was higher; either the trainers had had more success taming the horses, or the horses assigned were sounder and therefore more capable of being trained. Only three adult Brumbies didn't compete after the 150-day training period: Zali, one whose rider had been injured in an unrelated accident, and a horse that was injured on the way to the competition.

To see so many happy, well-adjusted horses at this competition was testament to the breed and to the way that the horses were prepared for the challenge. Of the three wild horse breeds we'd worked with, the Brumbies seemed to be the least affected by the transition from wild to captive, and we honestly believed that the passive trapping followed by the months of transition time at the Brumby sanctuary were major factors: the horses were mentally ready for training and were sounder than their New Zealand and American counterparts. Also, the way the show was held, and the layout of the arena, stables and classes, were all designed to set the horses up to win. They were allowed to graze in the arena between classes and were stabled only metres away from where they were competing; most of the horses responded by behaving as if they were being ridden in their paddocks at home. It was an incredibly relaxing environment, and even the hundreds of spectators watching each class didn't distract from the peaceful setting.

AT THE CONCLUSION OF THE FREESTYLE, THE judges deliberated the scores and we rushed over to the Grand Pavilion for a book signing, then met at the ring to watch Vicki's final clinic. She was paired with two of Australia's leading trainers for a horsemanship feature, demonstrating how they would train young horses over a course of obstacles to foster their confidence.

Finally, it was time for the prize-giving; the trainers all led their Brumbies into the arena, standing side by side. It was remarkable that so many wild horses, ones that had been untouched just 150 days earlier, could be standing so quietly side by side. Even the older stallions were fine next to mares, and vice versa. We were incredibly impressed with the trainability, talent and nature of these very special Snowy Mountain ponies.

Shyla consistently placed in the top six in all of the classes, and I was thrilled to finish fifth overall. Amanda, who only a month before had been unsure whether she'd even get Ballarat ready in time to compete, was pleased with how well they'd performed, although they didn't place. However, that wasn't what she was worried about — as soon as the final scores had been announced it was straight into the auction; the most critical moment that would decide Ballarat's future.

Moza and her grandfather were standing at the ring waiting, and when it was time Amanda led Ballarat forward in front of the auctioneer. We all felt incredibly stressed; because Ballarat had been so well-behaved throughout the event, we'd had many people come up to us to express interest in purchasing her. We'd managed to divert most of the potential bidders, by showing them other Brumbies that better suited either their size or their needs — as Ballarat was one of the smallest of the Brumbies, very few people who approached us were size-appropriate. One grandmother, who wanted to bid on Ballarat for her granddaughter — who was both too big and also a very inexperienced rider — wasn't as easily dissuaded when we mentioned our concerns about the girl's suitability. And when we said that we'd already found her a small, young rider who was an approved bidder, she snappily replied that if they wanted Ballarat then they would just bid above everyone else.

Disheartened and hoping that she wasn't serious, Amanda stood holding Ballarat's lead while the bidding rose, and was hugely relieved when it stalled at just $1600 with Moza being announced as the winner; the 10-year-old had raised $2000 to bid with and we were relieved that the bidding stayed within her budget. Ballarat was one of the cheapest Brumbies auctioned that day, with some of the others selling for up to $5000, but she got the home we wanted. As soon as the auction was over, Moza dashed over to the stables to give us all a hug and then proudly loaded Ballarat onto a trailer to take home. Nina, who'd come over to watch Shyla perform and also to visit the Snowy Mountains to see where she'd been born, was also at the stables with us. It was incredibly special to have both of these young girls there, at the very beginning of the next chapter in the Brumbies' journey. Vicki, Amanda and I couldn't have been happier. We'd set out to save the lives of Brumbies and set them up for a better future, and not only had we done that but we'd also inspired two great girls to begin their own journey with these once-wild horses. We hoped that, like us, their childhood dreams would take them on their own journeys with horses, both wild and domestic.

EPILOGUE

Passing on the Baton

This book about the wild Brumbies is probably the most reflective of those I've written. As always, I haven't tried to gloss over the taming of wild horses, but instead have shared our journey to get to know these animals through the relationships we built while taming the special few entrusted to our care. It is important to document the good, the bad and the ugly, because we rarely learn if everything goes right.

We hope that the lessons of patience, dealing with disappointment, triumph and, foremost, putting the welfare of the horses first, shines through. Although this journey began because of the Australian Brumby Challenge, that in itself is not the most important factor. The end result can never be about a few moments in an arena; instead, it's about learning to put your horse's needs first, no matter the deadline or the pressure you might be under to perform. In a world where instant gratification is too often sought, it's about understanding that compassion and patience are sometimes the most important qualities in life; not masking problems to present a horse in an arena, but instead building a foundation for that horse to lead a successful, full and happy life.

Because of their size, the Brumbies inspired in us a passion to share our knowledge with a younger generation and, in hindsight, it's been a blessing. Observing the world and taming wild ponies through the eyes of children allowed us, in a way, to re-live our own childhood. Every insight shared and lesson taught to Gaia, Shanti, Nina and Lily reminded us of our own experiences taming our first wild ponies 20 years ago; although we ourselves learnt through trial and error, and didn't have someone to guide us, the same feel and understanding on how to read a horse's body language was learnt from a young age and has stood us in good stead, developing us into the horsewomen we are today.

We have no doubt that the four young New Zealanders that shared the Brumbies' adventures with us have a very promising future, as does Moza over in Australia. Never have we seen such talented, determined and positive go-getters who simply don't understand the meaning of the word no and are willing to give everything a go, who are committed to doing everything to the highest standard possible and always have a smile on their faces. As children we were taught that anything was possible if we were willing to put the time into making it happen and were prepared to make sacrifices while wholeheartedly chasing our dreams. It's been so rewarding seeing these attributes shine through in the riders we mentor.

After the Australian Brumby Challenge, Moza and Ballarat's journey began, as did Shyla's ongoing adventures with Nina. There is no denying we were unsure how the ponies would transition to constantly being ridden and cared for by 10- and 11-year-old riders, and in both countries we had plans in place if the ponies needed further training. To our absolute delight both Moza and Nina have been able to continue producing their young Brumbies themselves, growing together and developing a solid relationship.

In Australia, Ballarat and Moza have gone on to enjoy a well-rounded lifestyle, including trekking out in National Parks, swimming in lakes, attending Pony Club and competing in showjumping events to 60 cm, most recently placing 10th of 50 ponies at the Victorian State Interschool Championships. A remarkable achievement for a young Brumby who nine months earlier had been running wild, and a real testament to how patiently Moza has continued to produce her over the past five months.

Likewise, Gaia and Shanti's work with the Kaimanawas, then the Brumbies alongside Nina and Lily, has set them up for a lifetime of success in their equestrian pursuits. The growth we've seen in our young protégés over the past year, from their horsemanship and right through to their showjumping, has come about through hours of mentoring with the wild ponies, jumping lessons, goal setting and endless hard work. We only wish we could have had the opportunities that they have had over the past year and are thankful we are in a position to be able to share our passion with them.

Since Shyla returned to New Zealand she has continued to become the ultimate second pony for Nina. At home they most often ride out bareback, cantering up the hills or riding down the road in a halter; simply having fun and building confidence together. Frequently over summer they came to stay, joining us for days, or sometimes a full week to ride alongside us, taking their ponies swimming in the river, out on the farm or having jumping lessons on the arena. Just a few months after Shyla returned from Australia, she and Nina competed at their first Ribbon Day, winning and placing in many classes, before going on to compete in the Show Hunter Winter Series — I couldn't be more proud of how Nina continues to put the best interests of Shyla first and we are excited to see what their future holds.

I hope these young riders realise how much we have also learnt from mentoring them, how many good memories it brings back from our own childhood, and how much they have encouraged us to continue to share everything our love of horses has taught us. If we can educate and inspire people of every generation to be better horse-owners, there will be a lot of grateful horses in this world. Our challenge to each of you is to always seek knowledge, strive to be better, strive to do better and live life to the full.

As for the wild Brumbies still roaming free across Australia, their future hangs in the balance. The one thing we are sure of, in any country, is that if wild horses aren't valued locally, no one can help them. I hope people open their hearts to these wild horses so they too can experience firsthand how remarkable they are, not only for their outstanding ability to thrive in domestication but also how much they can teach us along the way. While we understand that at times there is a need to cull, we strongly believe that this needs to be done in a humane manner — both for the welfare of the horses and also so that it doesn't become one of the biggest mass slaughters of wild horses in the modern age. From working with wild horses in three different countries, we also know first-hand the importance of preserving viable herds for people to both enjoy and learn from, not only through the domestication process but also from observing them in the wild.

GLOSSARY

AGEING — The process of estimating a horse's age by inspecting its teeth.

ARENA — An enclosed area for training or riding horses.

BIT — An object, usually a metal bar, placed in the mouth of a horse. It is held on by a bridle and used with reins to direct and guide the animal.

BRONCO — When a horse tries to buck off its rider.

COLIC — Any of several painful digestive disorders, usually involving intestinal displacement or blockage. It is a leading cause of death among horses.

CONDITION — An evaluation of a horse's overall weight and health.

CONFORMATION — The shape and proportion of a horse's body.

CONTACT — Contact is the minimum amount of feel on the reins required to evoke a change in a horse's speed or direction.

CROSSBAR — A jump formed by two poles crossing to form an 'X'.

CRUSH — A strongly built yard for holding horses or other livestock safely while they are examined, marked or given veterinary treatment.

DOUBLE CLEAR — When a horse or pony jumps clear in both the qualifying and jump off rounds of a showjumping competition.

FORMATION RIDING — A group of horses and riders (usually four) performing choreographed manoeuvres to music.

GALVAYNE'S GROOVE — Galvayne's groove is located on the lateral surface of the upper third incisor and is useful in ageing older horses. It appears first near the gum line at about 10 years of age. The groove extends halfway down the tooth at 15 years, and all the way down the tooth by 20 years. By approximately 25 years, Galvayne's groove is halfway gone, and by 30 years, it has disappeared completely.

GELDED/GELDING — Castration/A castrated male horse of any age.

HALTER — A device made of rope or leather straps that fits around the head or neck of a horse and is used to lead or secure the animal.

HANDS — A measurement of the height of a horse. It was originally taken from the size of a grown man's hand, but is now standardised to 4 inches. The measurement is usually taken from the ground to the withers.

HEAD-SHY — A horse that fears movement near its head, or being touched on the head.

LATERAL WORK — Movements made by a horse where the animal is moving in a direction other than straight forward.

LUNGE — To work or train a horse at the end of a long rope, teaching it to exhibit good ground manners and to exercise it when not ridden.

MARE — A mature female horse, usually four years of age or older. Also any female horse that has given birth, regardless of her age.

MOUTHING — Getting an untrained horse to accept a bit.

NAP — Refuse to go forward.

OXER — A jump with two verticals close together to create a wider jump.

POLL — The point immediately behind, or right between, the ears of a horse.

PONY (vs horse) — A pony is a member of the horse breed that typically measures to 14.2 hands high (148 centimetres) or shorter.

SHOW HUNTER — A type of horse and horse-show competition, judged on the horse's movement, manners and way of going, particularly over fences. A hunter should be graceful and maintain a long frame on the flat and while jumping fences.

SOUND/SOUNDNESS — A sound horse is one that has no lameness or illness.

SPLINTS — Ossification (additional bone growth) of the second and fourth metacarpal or metatarsal bones in the leg of the horse, which often occurs after impact injury to the area (such as from a kick).

STOCK HORSE — (1) A horse or pony used in herding cattle. (2) A recognised breed which has been specially bred for Australian conditions.

SURCINGLE — A piece of training equipment which goes around the barrel (middle part) of the horse. It is usually padded at the top, and is buckled around the horse to get a horse used to wearing a saddle, or to secure a saddle blanket to make a horse more comfortable when ridden bareback.

WALER — A breed of riding horse that developed from those brought to colonial Australia.

WEANLING — A young horse that has been weaned, usually between six months and a year.

WITHERS — The ridge between the shoulder blades of a horse. It is the tallest point of the horse's body and is the standard place to measure their height.

WOLF TEETH — Small, non-functional teeth that can cause problems for the domestic horse due to their location in the 'bars' of the mouth (the area between the incisors and the grinding cheek teeth) where the bit sits.

YEARLING — A horse between one and two years old.

ACKNOWLEDGEMENTS

Thank You

We were once told it takes a village to save a Brumby, and this couldn't have been more true in our experience. Our adventures with the Brumbies, more than any other wild horse breed, was a true team effort due to the costs involved and also their small stature. By working together we ensured the best possible outcome for these horses, and we are so thankful to everyone who aided us in their journey.

Our biggest thanks goes to Isuzu Utes New Zealand. Your belief in us has been inspiring and we are honoured to be part of the Isuzu family — the D-Max and MU-X are always in the middle of our adventures and we can't imagine life without them. Thank you for supporting our work with the Brumbies; everything that has happened in these pages was only made possible thanks to your support and generosity.

During our lives we have been privileged to cross paths with some amazing people who have a genuine love of horses. Colleen O'Brien, the president of the Victorian Brumby Association and our host during our time in Australia, is one of them. A huge thank you to you and your beautiful family for everything you do for the wild Brumbies . . . the horses are lucky to have you.

To Gaia and Shanti, thank you for reminding us of ourselves when we were your age. You are incredibly special and talented young riders and will go very far in life. Your innate feel and passion for horses can't be denied and we consider it a real privilege to have had your help with the Kaimanawas, Brumbies and showjumpers — you are so much fun to have around. Of course a special mention to your beautiful mother, Anna. Thank you for sharing your kids with us — you should be incredibly proud of them.

To Nina, thank you for loving Shyla as much as I do. It makes me so happy to have her back in New Zealand and to see her most weeks when you come out to ride. You are doing a fabulous job producing her, and every time I see you ride I am blown away by your talent — not only with horses but also your writing. To Lily, although you don't appear often in this book, you are equally valued; your help with the showjumpers has been amazing — it is a pleasure watching you develop into a kind, thoughtful and extremely talented young equestrian.

To La'Moza and your amazing mum Danielle — we feel so privileged to have crossed paths with you. Thank you for giving Ballarat a dream home. It's not often you find 10-year-olds so talented and willing to give a young pony a go. Your partnership with Ballarat has been one of the biggest highlights of our journey with the Brumbies; we eagerly await every update of her adventures and are so thankful she continues to have such a diverse and adventurous life with you.

To both Dans at Double Dan Horsemanship, thank you. Dan Steers for introducing us to Moza and helping us find Ballarat the perfect home, for lending us horses during our time at Equitana and for having Vicki for a week's training in the lead-up to Road to the Horse 2017 — we are beyond grateful for the friendship and hospitality you showed. Dan James, thanks for making us feel welcome and recognising in Vicki a talent with young horses. She was honoured to have you scout her for Road to the Horse 2017 as the very first English-style trainer to compete. Thank you for having her at your property in Kentucky in the week leading up to the event — her win at the World Championships of Colt Starting wouldn't have been possible without you.

Thank you to every Brumby supporter who crossed our paths. A special mention to the wonderful Brumby groups that make up the Australian Brumby Alliance — although you don't always see eye-to-eye, you are all passionately fighting for the same cause and the wild horses are lucky to have such a committed community.

To our fellow trainers in the Australian Brumby Challenge, thank you for opening your homes and your hearts to the wild Brumbies you trained — they quite literally owe you their lives. To the Victorian Brumby Association, thank you for everything you have done to ensure the success of showcasing the trainability of wild Brumbies to such a huge audience. The Australian Brumby Challenge was one of the most inspiring displays of horsemanship we have ever seen and you should be incredibly proud of how many happy and well-adjusted horses there were because of your tireless efforts.

Of course we can't forget the special horses that crossed our paths. Thank you Arana for reminding us that some wild horses will always have a better quality of life if left free to roam, and Shyla, Ballarat and Zali for trusting us and embracing the changes you faced. All three of you have such beautiful souls and it has been a pleasure watching you transform from your wild states. Being able to compare three different breeds of wild horses and also domestic horses has been the opportunity of a lifetime, and it's taught us so much. We are so grateful to all the wild horses for what they have taught us, for the people we have met because of them, and for the insights they have given us about horse behaviour.

A very heartfelt thank you must of course go to Argo, one of the most noble and intelligent wild horses that we were honoured to have as part of our lives, however briefly — you meant the world to us. Your time with us was far too short and we miss you every day. Thank you for everything you taught us and the special place you continue to hold in our hearts. We loved you deeply and continue to grieve you — may you gallop the plains once again with Major and the rest of the horses we have lost.

Most importantly, a huge thanks goes to my sisters and the team that works with us behind the scenes; our parents for letting us run riot as children and make our own adventures, encouraging our intuition, Kiwi ingenuity and intelligence. To Paula for holding the fort and managing our horses while we were based offshore, and to Alexa for your witty humour and friendship during our travels. It's an honour to do life alongside you all and we appreciate everything you do.